I0558013

THE TRØNDERS

A Quirky Guide to Trondheim, Trønderland and
Its People

Tania Winther

Staten House

Copyright © Tania Winther, 2nd Edition, 2025.

The Trønders: A Quirky Guide to Trondheim, Trønderland and Its People.

Imprint: Staten House

ISBN: 979-8-89778-4868 Paperback

All rights reserved.

No portion of this book may be reproduced in any form without written permission from the publisher or author, except as permitted by U.S. copyright law. All words and illustrations are by the author. Some of the illustrations are created with assistance from AI tools, such as fotor, photoshop, Rebel four, Coral painter blending hand drawings with technology and creativity to bring the visuals to life. I use a wide range of different techniques when creating. Please note that my drawings, made with ink, markers and pencil, are not exact representations of the places in Trondheim in real life, they're my humorous take on them.

www.atelierwinther.no

CONTENTS

Dedication   1

Disclaimer   2

2. Introduction   5

3. Where is Trøndelag? Who are the Trønders?   8

4. Trøndere are everywhere   13

6. Everyday Life and Quirks   15

7. Trønder Culture   17

8. Typical Trøndersk   21

9. Humor - Dry, Deadpan, and Delightfully Sarcastic   24

10. The Unspoken Rule for Norwegians   26

12. The Trønders' Mysterious Dialect – A Crash Course   30

13. The Art of Small Talk (or Lack Thereof)   33

14. Æ E I A Æ Å   34

15. The Trønder 'Language'   35

16. The Trønders' Mysterious Dialect – A Crash Course (continues)   38

18. Social Interactions and Relationships   47

19. Food and Traditions   56

21. Trondheim Through the Ages – The Historical Heart of Norway   61

22. The City That Rose (and Burned, and Rose Again)   63

23. Myths, Tales and Legends   67

24. The Trøndelag Bucket List – How to Spend Your Time in Trondheim Like a True Trønder   71

25. Local Traditions and Celebrations – Where the Past Meets the Present   80

26. Skiing and Nature   84

28. Trønders' Relationship with Nature – It's Personal   87

29. Fjellvettreglene (The Mountain Safety Rules)   91

30. World Ski Championship 2025 – Trondheim's Time to Shine (Or Freeze)   94

31. After-Ski (and what it really is?)   98

33. Trøndelag – Where Everyone Is Low-Key Famous   102

34. Famous Trønders – Proof That You Can Be a Superstar Even if You Hate Small Talk   104

35. More Trønder Celebrities – Because Trøndelag Is Basically Norway's Talent Factory   108

36. Old Nidaros: Norway's Not-So-Secret Pretender to the Throne   115

37. Trøndere vs. the Rest of Norway: A Playful Comparison   119

38. Trondheim Rising to International Fame   123

39. Afterword   126

40. Bonus: Essential Trønder Experiences   129

41. The Author   130

42. Dig Deeper: Books & Resources   131

43. The Unofficial Law of Trønderism   134

Dedication

To my beloved children, family and ancestors, whose stories and spirits inspired this book.

A special thank you to Lorelou Desjardins (A Frog in the Fjord) for her invaluable help and kindness, and for believing in my book from the start.

Bodil Mostad Olsen, for her Trøndersk patience and guidance, and for her expertise in book design and book covers.

To Per Arne, a Trøndersk artist and gallery owner, whose encouragement and creative suggestions have inspired and guided me.

And to all the Trønders who have taught me the rich traditions, culture and language that have become so close to my heart.

This book is for you all.

DISCLAIMER

A Nod to the Richness of Trøndersk

The Trønder language is as vast and varied as Trøndelag itself. Stretching far and wide, Trøndelag encompasses a rich history of accents, dialects, and unique expressions that make Trøndersk one of Norway's most distinctive linguistic treasures.

In writing this book, I recognize that it is impossible to capture the full richness and diversity of Trøndersk vocabulary. What you will find here are carefully selected words, phrases, bits and bobs drawn from various parts of Trøndelag, not just Trondheim.

This book is a tribute to the language and culture of the region, but it is by no means a comprehensive linguistic guide. Instead, it is a playful, affectionate exploration meant to entertain, inform, and celebrate the quirky and heartwarming essence of Trøndersk.

The myths, tales and legends are stories I have picked up from various people over the years.

My hope is that these snippets serve as a lighthearted introduction to the language and culture of Trøndelag, while honoring the vastness and richness that cannot be fully captured in a single volume.

"This book became more than a guide. It became a bridge. A way to decode Trønder life for others while deepening my own understanding of it."

-T.

Introduction

Welcome to Trønderland!

Welcome to the land of Trøndere: A people with a history as rich as their language is baffling. In this guide, I'll take you through the strange, wonderful, and sometimes downright confusing world of Trøndere and its locals, with observations from the capital of Trøndelag -Trondheim - and a few other places in the region. From their talking in vowels, to their unique words that seem like they were invented after a long night out, you're in for a treat. Or, at the very least, a good laugh. If you've ever wondered what it's like to get lost in translation, where a simple "hello" can sound like a growl and everyday phrases leave you scratching your head, then Trønderland is the place for you. As we look into the heart of Trøndelag, we'll explore not just the city's breathtaking fjords and colorful wooden houses, but also the quirks of a people who seem to have mastered the art of speaking in code. You'll learn how to blend in (or stand out) with their accent, navigate their love of understatement, and maybe even make sense of why "uff da" is both an exclamation and a state of mind. Prepare yourself for an adventure like no other, where the history is serious, but everything else is up for interpretation. Because, after all, being a Trønder is as much about attitude as it is about place. So, grab your coffee (or your *karsk*), buckle up, and let's take a plunge into the most linguistically bewildering, culturally rich corner of Norway, and if you're reading this, you've either found yourself in Trondheim or the outskirts, wondering what makes this place tick, or you're just curious about the people who call themselves Trønders. This book emerged organically from my work with newcomers to Trondheim. Initially, it was a practical guide, something I created to help those I was working for understand local customs, social norms, and the unspoken rules of life here. But as I wrote, I realized I was also making sense of it all for myself. Having spent years abroad and working with foreigners in Trondheim, I had firsthand experience of the cultural gaps and the challenges of integration.

This book became more than a guide: it became a bridge... a way to decode Trønder life for others while deepening my own understanding of it. I come from a somewhat confusing cultural blend, having grown up in so many places that each one has left me with a slightly different accent and a never-ending sense of jet lag. Yet, despite (or maybe because of) that *Third Culture Kid* (TCK) syndrome, my Norwegian heritage somehow reeled me in again and again. I moved here, moved away again, then came back—and the cycle kept repeating until I finally settled down, started a family, and jumped headfirst into the adventure of becoming (or at least understanding) a Trønder.

Frankly, becoming a full-fledged Trønder doesn't exactly happen overnight.

I had plenty of awkward attempts at blending in, and sometimes I failed—spectacularly. But through each and every stumble and bemused smile, I learned to adjust, accept the culture (even the strange bits), and—most importantly—to laugh along the way (and I'm still learning).

On top of that, I'm generally a bit culturally confused!

So where do I actually come from? Where do I belong?

Only a *Third Culture Kid* can understand the complexity—and maybe they're just as puzzled as I am!

Anyway, I'm thrilled to have you along for the ride, so let's uncover the beauty, the humor, and the heart of Trønderland together!

- The Term Third Culture Kid (Often abbreviated TCK) describes children and young people who have spent a significant part of their upbringing in a country other than their parent's home country and their own passport country.

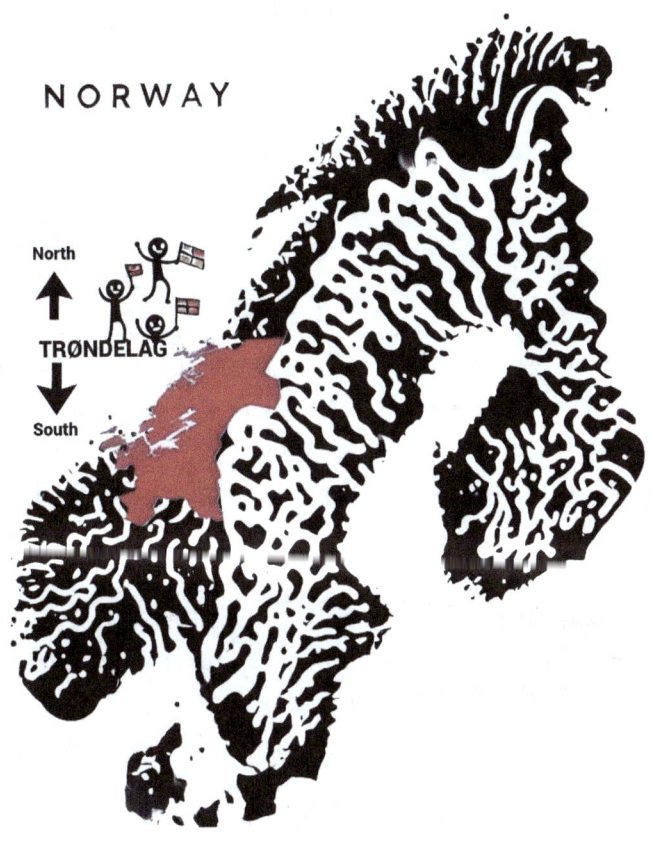

WHERE IS TRØNDELAG? WHO ARE THE TRØNDERS?

Where is Trøndelag Located?

Trøndelag is a central region of Norway. "Trøndelag stretches from the southern border near Dovre and Dovrefjell(mountain range) in Innlandet county, to the northern part of Rørvik." It's strategically placed at the heart of the country, making it both a geographic and cultural crossroads. The region consists of two 'counties', South-Trøndelag and North-Trøndelag, which were merged in 2018 to form Trøndelag county. Trondheim, the region's crown jewel, serves as its unofficial capital.

Trondheim: A city like no other (and that's not just bragging)

Trondheim is the third largest city in Norway, and is the proud capital of Trøndelag and the spiritual home of the Viking era. It's a place where history, culture, and an accent thicker than 'brunost' (brown cheese) collide in a manner so distinct, you'll never quite recover.

Who exactly are the Trønders?

The Trønders are the proud inhabitants of Trøndelag. Known for their robustness, dry humor, and a no-nonsense attitude, they are a blend of modern Norwegians and their Viking ancestors. Historically, Trønders played a crucial role in Norway's Viking age, with Trondheim (then Nidaros) as the Viking capital and a central hub for trade and exploration.

Trønders are also famous for their distinct dialect, or language if you will. Trøndersk, and their ability to adapt to Trøndelag's famously erratic weather. They're community oriented, often gathering for activities like fishing, hiking, and the occasional dugnad (a communal work effort), all while sipping black coffee strong enough to double as jet fuel.

Do Trønders exist outside of Trøndelag?

Absolutely. While Trønders are deeply rooted in Trøndelag, they've been known to wander. You'll find them sprinkled across Norway and even around the world, often carrying their distinctive dialect and humor with them like a badge of honor. Oslo, Norway's capital, has a fair share of transplanted Trønders, many of whom gather in tight-knit groups to lament the lack of proper coffee and weather complaints that measure up to Trondheim standards.

Internationally, Trønders can be found in surprising places, from the fjords of Iceland to the streets of Brooklyn, New York. They're drawn by opportunities for education, work, or just the chance to prove that their accent can baffle foreigners just as effectively as it does other Norwegians. Regardless of where they go, they remain unmistakably Trønder, greeting the world with a stoic "Heia!" and a love for fishing metaphors.

Trønder Quirks

Trønders are a breed apart. They'll greet you with a booming "Heia" or "Hei hei"! Once you have greeted them first, mind you! Their stoic expressions hide a wellspring of deadpan humor that'll leave you wondering if they're joking or offering heartfelt life advice. Spoiler: It's both.

For example, a Trønder might tell you, "Det e bæst å itj prøv så gæli. Livet e litt som å fiske; du får berre det du får," (It's best not to try too hard. Life is like fishing; you only get what you get.) Whether this is wisdom or resignation is unclear, but it's undeniably very Trønder.

The Accent: A language course you didn't ask for

Trondheim's linguistic gift to the world is the Trøndersk accent. It's not so much a dialect as it is a lifestyle, a language of its own. You'll quickly notice that Trønders favor short, punchy words, as if vowels are a luxury they can't always afford. For instance:

"Hvordan går det?" (How's it going?) becomes "Korleis gå're?"

"Hva sa du?" (What did you say?) transforms into "Ka'd sa?"

But the real linguistic adventure comes in deciphering slang. Words like 'sopinn' (hungry) and 'ka' (what), add local flavor that'll either endear you to the Trønders or leave you hopelessly confused. Either way, you're in for a good time.

The Holy Grail: The "Trønder Combo"

If you're looking to truly blend in, you'll need to master the "Trønder Combo," a trifecta of behaviors that will cement your place among the locals:

Hold a stoic face: Laughing too much or showing excessive enthusiasm will make you stick out like a sore thumb. Practice your neutral expression in the mirror until even you aren't sure if you're happy.

Carry a fishing rod (Optional): Whether you're heading to the fjord or just walking through the city center, a fishing rod adds instant credibility. Bonus points if you've actually caught a fish. Double bonus points if you caught it in a suit.

Drink coffee like It's a sport: Trønders are powered by coffee, ideally consumed black and in quantities that would concern most health professionals.

The Weather: A personality test in disguise

Trondheim's weather is best described as "unpredictable" and worst described as "an affront to all plans." Locals, however, take it in stride. A common Trønder saying goes, "Det finns itj dårlig vær, bare dårlig klær," (There's no bad weather, only bad clothing). This phrase is repeated so often, it might as well be printed on the city's flag.

In Trøndelag, it's not unusual to experience all four seasons in a single afternoon. This keeps Trønders on their toes and has led to a unique fashion trend best described as "functional layering meets Viking pragmatism."

Trønder Humor: Dry as the arctic wind

Trønder humor is subtle, sharp, and often so dry you'll need a glass of water just to keep up.

Food: More than just survival

No discussion of Trondheim is complete without mentioning its culinary scene. From the traditional sodd (a hearty mutton soup) to modern fine dining, Trondheim caters to every palate. However, don't be surprised if a Trønder insists that nothing beats a "real" meal of bread, butter, and spread (*matpakke*) and coffee.

Pro tip: If a Trønder offers you fermented fish, just smile and say, "Kanskje seinar" (Maybe later). It's the polite way out.

Final Thoughts: Embrace the chaos

Visiting Trøndelag and mingling with Trønders is less about understanding and more about accepting. Whether it's the weather, the accent, or the humor, there's something about this region that grows on you, like moss on a Viking helmet.

Trøndelag is like the sweet spot on Norway's map right where the rock 'n' roll vibes are strong! Since Norway's map resembles a guitar, Trøndelag became the rock star region, strumming the perfect chords of oil wealth and stunning fjords. Trøndelag, the ultimate rock zone of the country where the riffs are as epic as the landscapes!

Note! Grab your rain jacket, practice your deadpan face, and get ready to experience a city that's equal parts history, charm, and lovable eccentricity.

TRØNDERE ARE EVERYWHERE

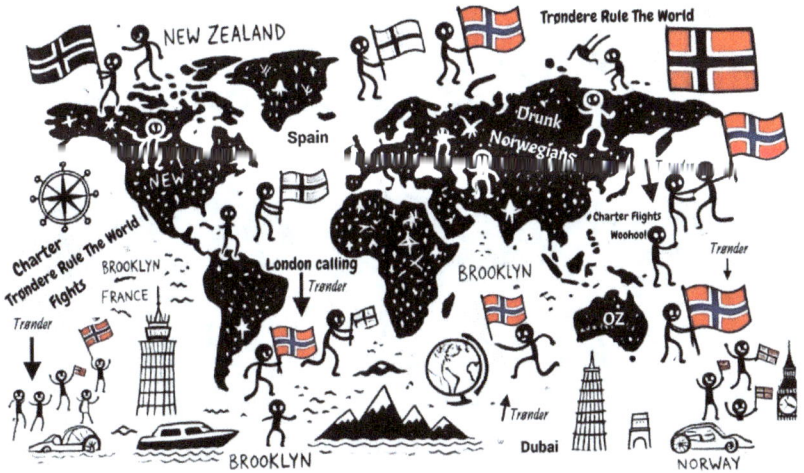

Trøndere Rule The World

"In Trøndersk, you can say 'hæ' without anyone taking it the wrong way, because they know you're just trying to understand the world in Trøndersk."

–T (Inspired by Norwegians)

EVERYDAY LIFE AND QUIRKS

Everyday Life and Quirks
Explore the idiosyncrasies of a Trønders lifestyle. How they behave, socialize, and approach situations.

TRØNDER CULTURE

Where Understatement is an Art Form, and "Uff Da" Says It All

If there's one thing you need to know about Trønder culture, it's that Trønders have perfected the art of saying a lot without saying much at all. While other Norwegians are busy with polite small talk, Trønders are out here giving a shrug, an "uff da," and somehow expressing the entire spectrum of human emotion in those two syllables. If you ask a Trønder how their day's been, don't expect a story, expect an "tja nja" (which means everything and nothing depending on how it's said).

Weather: The True Trønder Obsession

Forget politics or celebrity gossip, weather is the only topic that matters in Trondheim Rain, sun, hail, or snow, no day is complete without at least five weather-related comments. And if you think that sounds boring, you've clearly never experienced the roller-coaster that is Trønder weather. A typical day might start with sunshine, only to switch to sleet, then a brief snowstorm, and then, just for fun, a rainbow. It's practically a sport to predict the next weather phenomenon. Hence, the national pastime of Trondheim: weather complaints.

Nature: Love It, Respect It, Complain About It

Trønders might grumble about the weather, but deep down, they love the great outdoors. Hiking, skiing, fishing, it's all part of the package. But don't let this fool you into thinking they're the chatty, cheerful outdoor types. A Trønder's idea of a good hike is to walk silently for hours, stop at a mountain peak, grunt "bra utsikt" (nice view), then continue walking in stoic silence. After all, who needs words when you've got fjords?

Small Talk: The Trønder Challenge

Small talk in Trondheim is a test of endurance. Once you can survive the blank stares and awkward pauses, you've officially been accepted into the fold. The trick? Less is more. The Trønder conversational style involves dropping cryptic one-liners like "ska du på hytta?" (Are you going to the cabin?) or "jaja, sånn e d" (Yeah yeah, that's how it is).

The Mysterious Power of "Uff Da"

If you hear a Trønder mutter "uff da," don't panic, it's not a cry for help. It's just the most versatile phrase in the Trønder language. Bad weather? "Uff da." Someone stepped on your foot? "Uff da." Life is going great but you just don't feel like showing excitement? Yep, "uff da" works for that too. It's practically a Jedi mind trick. Once you master it, you'll be one step closer to understanding the true power of Trønder understatement.

Pro tip: If they start talking about fishing or their latest cabin renovation, you're in, you've broken through the ice.

'Bartebyen': (The Moustache City.)

Trondheim is often referred to as 'the moustache city'. This is due to an old stereotype that men from Trondheim and the Trøndelag region generally have moustaches. This idea likely originated because moustaches, were among men in the region, once a popular style, especially in the 70s and 80s. While it is not so common anymore, the term has stuck and is now used as a humorous and somewhat affectionate nickname for the city.

Pro tip: If you are lucky, you might still spot a busdriver or taxi driver living up to the reputation with long moustaches.

Strange Oddities with Trøndere

Let me warn you about a little quirk when it comes to dining with Trøndere. If you bring wine to a dinner party, don't assume it's a gift for the host. Oh no, my friend, it's more like a loan. You see, when the party winds down, the giver of the wine will quite likely want to take it back, even if it's half-drunk by the end of the night. Yes, you read that right. I'm not joking! Don't say I didn't warn you. Now, don't mistake this for rudeness or stinginess, it's really just a reflection of the deeply practical mindset of these people. In their eyes, this isn't about gifts or gestures. Instead, it's more like an unspoken rule, born from a culture where every resource, even a bottle of wine, is respected and accounted for. Remember, it's not really that long ago that Norway struck oil and became one of the riches countries in the world!

And if you're thinking, "Well, I'll just bring my own wine when we go out to dinner at a restaurant," think again! Trondheim, and Norway in general, has something called Vinmonopolet, the Wine Monopoly. It's the government's way of saying, "You shall not pass!" to anyone hoping to BYO. So, if you're craving a nice glass of wine with your meal, you'll have to trust the restaurant's selection or make a stop at Vinmonopolet beforehand. Many Norwegians still retain values rooted in humility and prudence, even as the nation has grown remarkably affluent. This can been shown in the way they live and where they live. However, I dare say, this is changing drastically too, these days. Yet this shift is not without tension. While some are embracing a new, cosmopolitan standard of living, many still carry that ingrained sense of thrift and reserve. It's a unique paradox, the wealth is there, but so is the old habit of modesty. And while Trøndere may still hesitate to let go of a half-drunk bottle of wine (or aquevit), they're just as likely to be planning their next getaway or investing in a mountain cabin. Norway is in transition, and it's fascinating to watch how the past and present interact in the everyday choices people make.

The Paradox of Dugnad

Dugnad is one of those truly great things about Norwegian life, especially here in Trondheim. It's this brilliant community spirit where neighbors come together to rake leaves, shovel snow, or paint the local playground like it's the most natural thing in the world. Everybody chips in, no questions asked. You can go years without exchanging more than a nod with the person next door, but when dugnad day arrives, suddenly everyone's out there in matching reflective vests, working like old pals.

But here's where it gets weird. The second dugnad is over? Boom. It's back to business as usual, polite but distant. Striking up a chat with your neighbors or, heaven forbid, trying to start a conversation at the supermarket? Absolutely not. If you dare to say something like, "Oh, nice weather today," to the person next to you at the checkout, you're basically marking yourself crazy. You'll get that polite but terrified smile, and they'll retreat faster than you can say vær så god.

So while dugnad brings people together in this beautifully organized chaos, the idea of casually talking to someone outside that context can feel borderline scandalous. It's as if Trøndere have a social switch that only turns on when manual labor is involved. The rest of the time, interaction can feel strictly off-limits, not out of rudeness, but out of an innate shyness and a deep-seated respect for personal space. They're simply reluctant to impose, not wanting to bother anyone unless there's a clear reason. It's a cultural quirk that's both endearing and puzzling, and perhaps one I'll never fully solve!

Adding to this, there's the undeniable factor of winter depression. The long, dark months can dampen even the brightest of spirits, so people often retreat into their own worlds. But the moment the sun returns, you'll see a transformation; suddenly, people are smiling and even greeting you on the street. It's as if the sunshine itself flips a collective switch, and a warmth that's been hibernating for months starts to thaw.

And if you've managed to learn a bit of trøndersk, with its unique dialect, quirky expressions, and all, you're in for a real treat. Cracking the Trønder dialect is like a secret handshake, an instant ticket to being part of the conversation. Once you're "in," you'll find that Trøndere have a lot to say, especially if there's a bit of sunshine to go around.

Typical Trøndersk

A typical "Trønder" is often characterized by a laid-back, friendly demeanor and a strong regional identity. Trønders tend to take pride in their dialect, which is distinct and filled with peculiar words and phrases. They often have a dry, understated sense of humor, and their speech can come across as straightforward, sometimes even a bit blunt. Trøndere are proud of several key aspects of their identity and heritage. From their dialect to their viking heritage, to the medieval Nidaros Cathedral, to their local football (soccer) team, Rosenborg. Their local, traditional food, such as 'sodd', (a meat and vegetable stew, both served at funerals as well as weddings!)

Historically, Trondheim has been a center of Norwegian culture and religion, but the people today are often seen as pragmatic and down-to-earth. Many Trønders enjoy the outdoors, taking part in activities like skiing, hiking, and fishing, as the region is surrounded by nature.

In terms of appearance, there's no single look, but you might encounter Trønders who embrace traditional Norwegian woollen sweaters ("kofte") in winter or show an affinity for Viking history, as Trondheim was once the Viking capital of Norway. The typical Trønder is also known for a strong sense of community, often proud of their heritage and eager to keep their local traditions alive.

Giving a compliment to a Trønder can be like tossing a tennis ball to a cat, there's a good chance it'll just get ignored or batted back at you with a look of mild suspicion. Picture this: You say, "Wow, this food is amazing!" and the Trønder stares at you, squints, and says,

"Åh, det e' no itj nåkka spesielt" ("Oh, it's nothing special") Or you tell them, "You did a great job with that project!" and they'll probably mutter, "Ahh, anyone could've done it..." as they pretend they barely put any effort into it. It's not that they don't appreciate the praise, they'd just rather wrestle a moose than admit it. Complimenting a Trønder is like playing a game of emotional ping-pong where the goal is for you to take the compliment back. FYI! It's less about rudeness and more about a cultural inclination towards modesty and self-deprecation. So, while Trøndere appreciates compliments, they might show it in a subtler way!

Humor - Dry, Deadpan, and Delightfully Sarcastic

The Trønders have mastered the art of delivering jokes with such a straight face that you might not realize you've been laughing until it's too late. Their humor isn't loud or exaggerated; instead, it's subtle, often delivered with a deadpan expression and a slight smirk, leaving you wondering whether they were serious or joking.

The Sarcastic "Javel"

One of the favorite tools in the Trønder humor arsenal is the word "javel," which technically means "yes" but is often used sarcastically. When you share something mildly surprising, you might get a "javel" or equally a "seriøs?" in return, delivered so dryly that you're left questioning whether they're agreeing or mocking you. That's the beauty of it: the humor is in the ambiguity.

The "Small Joys" Approach

Trønders love to poke fun at life's small absurdities. A rainy day in Trondheim? A Trønder might say with a completely straight face, "Perfect day for a picnic!" This kind of humor reflects their ability to find joy (or irony) in the mundane, making even the simplest conversations entertaining.

The " E det molig?" Approach In Trøndersk.

(literally "Is it possible?") is a classic expression often delivered with a straight face, but loaded with irony, disbelief, or mild frustration. It's the kind of phrase that can mean anything from "Are you kidding me?" to "I can't believe this nonsense." It's a simple phrase, but in true Trøndersk fashion, it's all about the tone—dry, unimpressed, and slightly amused.

It is definitely typical Trøndersk! Similar to "Seriøs?"(seriously?) or "går det an?" (Is that even a thing?) It can also be said with an exasperated tone to emphasize irritation.

THE UNSPOKEN RULE FOR NORWEGIANS

The Law of Jante (*Janteloven* in Norwegian) is a cultural concept in Scandinavia, often described as an informal set of societal norms that discourages individual success and boasting. It originated from the Danish-Norwegian author Aksel Sandemose's 1933 novel, *A Fugitive Crosses His Tracks* (*En flyktning krysser sitt spor*), which describes life in the fictional town of Jante. Here, Sandemose listed ten "laws" that capture a deeply ingrained Scandinavian mindset of humility, equality, and conformity.

**The main gist of Janteloven is: "Don't think you're better than anyone else."
Here are the ten rules:**

1. **Don't think you're something special.**

2. **Don't think you're as good as we are.**

3. **Don't think you're smarter than we are.**

4. **Don't convince yourself that you're better than we are.**

5. **Don't think you know more than we do.**

6. **Don't think you are more important than we are.**

7. **Don't think you are good at anything.**

8. **Don't laugh at us.**

9. **Don't think anyone cares about you.**

10. **Don't think you can teach us anything.**

These "laws" aren't literal laws but rather a way to explain a social attitude found in Scandinavia that values modesty, community, and downplays individual success. Although modern Scandinavians view the Law of Jante as old-fashioned, it's still part of the cultural mindset, so much so that you might see traces of it in how people react to success and self-promotion. For example, Trønders may joke about Janteloven when explaining why they don't boast or seek attention for personal achievements. Janteloven has pros and cons. On the one hand, it promotes equality and discourages arrogance, fostering a strong sense of community and fairness. On the other hand, it can sometimes stifle individual ambition, creativity, and the willingness to stand out.

Ah, Janteloven, that whispers in every Trønder's ear, "Don't think you're special." On the surface, it sounds noble: promoting equality, keeping egos in check, and ensuring no one starts strutting around like the king of the fjord. But for artists and entrepreneurs, it's like trying to paint with a wet blanket or sell your groundbreaking app while muttering, "It's nothing special, really."

Picture this: You're an artist, you've just unveiled a masterpiece, something so stunning it could rival the northern lights. But just as you're about to bask in your moment of glory, Janteloven leans over and says, "Don't think you're better than anyone else, da." Now you're sheepishly muttering, "Oh, it's just something I threw together. Not a big deal. Please don't look at it for too long."

But here's the kicker: while Janteloven might stifle your self-promotion, it has an unexpected side effect. Artists and entrepreneurs in Trondheim have mastered the art of humble bragging. They'll downplay their success with lines like, "It's just a little exhibition, at the Louvre, but whatever," or, "My company's doing okay... we're only expanding to five countries next year." It's a skill as Nordic as knitting sweaters in July.

In a way, Janteloven keeps things interesting. It forces artists to let their work speak louder than their words and entrepreneurs to build businesses so good they can't be ignored.

But sometimes, just sometimes, you wish Trondheimers could channel a little New York bravado and say, "Yes, I'm amazing, and so is my *lutefisk*-inspired NFT project. Deal with it."

Until then, Janteloven will remain the ultimate frenemy: keeping Trønders humble, grounded, and just slightly awkward about how brilliant they really are.

But wait, before you think Trondheim, and Norway for that matter, is all about modesty and self-deprecation, let's not forget about the outliers, the Janteloven escapees. Yes, we're looking at you, occasional do-gooders and know-it-all betters who somehow bypassed the humility filter. These are the people who march through life radiating unshakable confidence, leaving the rest of us wondering, "How did they slip through the cracks?"

They're the artist at the gallery opening who won't stop explaining why their painting is the pinnacle of modern expression. The entrepreneur pitching their product with the subtlety of a Viking raid: "This app will change humanity as we know it. You're welcome." These folks might be rare, but when they appear, they shine bright, like a disco ball at a funeral.

So yes, while Janteloven keeps most of us in check, the occasional escaped ego reminds us that confidence, like *lutefisk*, is best served in moderation. And really, isn't it comforting to know that even in the land of equality, there's always someone ready to disrupt the balance by declaring, "Actually, I do think I'm better than you, and here's why."

§ 9: Thou Shalt Believe Thou Art Northug

Forget the Jantelov, in Trøndelag, it is your **duty** to believe you are as fast, witty, and irresistibly charming as Petter Northug. Signing up for a ski race? Of course, you'll win (at least in the version of the story you tell later). Playing poker? Naturally, you have the same killer instinct as the king of the ski tracks. And most importantly, no matter how slow you actually ski, always remember: **it's the final sprint that counts**. A cheeky but affectionate nod to Northug's legacy!

"If a Trønder nods at you without saying anything,
don't panic. In many cases, it's all you'll get, and
it's all you need. Silence is simply a part of life"

– T

The Trønders' Mysterious Dialect – A Crash Course

If there's one thing that sets the Trønders apart from the rest of Norway, it's their dialect. Known for talking in vowels and for its rolling "r"s, Trøndersk sounds like someone decided to give Norwegian a twist and turn. For the untrained ear, it might seem as though you've stumbled upon a secret language, spoken only by those who live between the fjords and the mountains.

The key to understanding Trøndersk is to embrace the confusion. Words are often clipped, shortened, and sometimes, whole sentences seem to vanish into thin air. One distinctive feature is the heavy use of vowel sounds, often dropping consonants or softening them, which can make it sound like they're speaking mostly in vowels. Depending on where in the region of Trøndelag you are visiting, words and sentences tend to alter. So stay focused! Take for example "ka du sei?"—a phrase that technically means "what are you saying?" but is pronounced so quickly, you might miss it entirely. It's the kind of dialect that makes you realize communication is as much about attitude as it is about pronunciation. I have compiled a short list and tips for you here, of what I think are the most essential words and phrases to learn. Be aware. There are many more where they came from!

The first time I went on a date with a man from Nord-Trøndelag, I thought I had my Norwegian down. I mean, I speak the language, right? But then he started talking, and I realized I might as well have been listening to a secret code. "Æ sku'v de' no," he said, and I nodded, but in my head, I was thinking, What on earth did I just agree to? "Træn'du fløyti?" (Which I later learned means cream. As in do I want cream in my coffee!)

The more he spoke, the more I realized: Trøndersk is like an endless treasure hunt, and each area has its own set of amusing words and quirky expressions. It's like learning a new language every time you meet someone from a different part of the region! I came to a shocking realization that night, that no, I hadn't actually learned Trøndersk. It's going to take a lifetime, or more, to master all the variations of "å ska" and "fesk." And that's just the beginning!

Essential Tips:

Tip 1: Surviving Trøndelag: Mastering the Art of the Vowel Symphonies

Consonants are optional, vowels are king. When engaging in conversation with a trønder, you might notice that words sound more like melodic soundwaves than distinct syllables. It's not that trønders don't like consonants, it's just that they've evolved past the need for them.

Here's how to practice:

1. Loosen your jaw and let your vowels stretch out like you're trying to fill the fjords with your voice.

2. Omit half the consonants. Think of them as unnecessary baggage, you only need enough to keep the word recognizable (barely).

3. Add a sing-song quality to your tone. Trøndersk isn't spoken; it's *performed*.

Finally, remember: in Trøndelag, *less is more*. The fewer consonants you use, the more authentic you sound. So take a deep breath, embrace the vowels, and prepare to charm the locals with your newfound mastery of Trøndersk minimalism.

Tip 2: Embrace the R-roll.

The first hurdle for any non-Trønder trying to speak the dialect is the infamous "r." It's not just a letter in Trøndersk, it's a performance. When rolling the "r," imagine you're trying to start a lawnmower that's a bit rusty. You'll know you've mastered it when your throat feels a bit sore but your smile is wider.

Tip 3: Master the Art of Understatement.

In Trondheim, if you're expecting grand declarations of joy or despair, you're in the wrong place. The Trønders have perfected the art of understatement. No matter how amazing or catastrophic a situation might be, you'll often hear a calm and collected "nja, det går no bra," which loosely translates to "eh, it's fine." This can apply to anything from the weather to a personal crisis. When in doubt, underplay everything.

Tip 4: Uff da - The Universal Phrase.

"Uff da" is your new best friend. It's the phrase that fits almost every situation. Did you spill coffee on your shirt?" Uff da". Did you get caught in a sudden downpour without an umbrella? "Uff da". Trønders have a knack for using this simple phrase to convey frustration, empathy, or just the recognition that life is sometimes a bit of a mess. Don't confuse the phrase with a simular phrase; "**Uffa meg**". **It means an entirely different thing.** When a Trønder uses this phrase, note that they are really empathising with you, and are concerned, and care deeply, about what you are going through.

THE ART OF SMALL TALK (OR LACK THEREOF)

If you come from a culture where small talk flows freely, Trondheim might catch you off guard. Conversations here are direct and to the point. Trønders don't waste words; when they speak, it's usually with a purpose. But there's an art to the silence that follows, because, in Trondheim, silence is golden.

The Silent Nod

If a Trønder nods at you without saying anything, don't panic. In many cases, it's all you'll get, and it's all you need. A silent nod can mean "hello," "I agree," or even "goodbye." Silence isn't uncomfortable here, it's just part of life.

Yes means maybe, maybe means no.

Yes means maybe, maybe means no

Navigating a conversation with a Trønder can feel like reading between the lines. A "yes" doesn't always mean a firm commitment, and "maybe" is often just a polite way of saying no. There's a politeness in this indirectness, it allows people to avoid confrontation while still getting their point across.

THE TRØNDER 'LANGUAGE'

Take a deep dive into the distinctive language and dialect of the Trønders. Local slang, expressions, and pronunciation variations. Here you'll find examples of funny and unique phrases used by the locals.

The use of "æ"

Trøndersk is known for its frequent use of "æ". For example:

"æ ska dit" (I'm going there)

"ska vi færra?" (shall we go?)

This sound is distinctive and a significant part of the dialect.

Vowels

The Trønders tend to open up the vowels in words, creating a flowing and almost singing quality. This is especially evident in the words like:

"no/nå" (now)

"ska" (shall)

"te" (to)

You may find that some Trønders stretch the vowels in a way that makes them difficult to pinpoint exactly, giving the impression that they speak more in vowels than consonants. For example:

"Æ ska tæl by'n æ no". (I'm going to town now)

Diftongs

Trønders are fond of diphthongs, such as:

"hæinn" (he)

"læill" (still, its...)

Many words in the Trøndersk 'language' take on an "open" and melodic tone, which makes the language very vowel based.

THE TRØNDERS' MYSTERIOUS DIALECT - A CRASH COURSE (CONTINUES)

The Trøndersk Terminology - simply explained:

Trånnjæim - "Trondheim".

Klar - In proper Norwegian this word means "I am so ready". In Trøndersk it means: "I am so tired!"

Heisann - "Hello!"

Skål - "Cheers!"

Fær - "Leave or Go". In Norwegian: "Å dra".

Koinn - "To know". In Norwegian: "Å kunne".

Hannjhonnj i bannj - "A dog on a leash". In Norwegian: "En hannhund i bånd".

Jæven - In English: "Gosh". In Norwegian: "Jøss".

Må itj fårrå nålles - "Don't go anywhere". Or actually, it could also mean: "Come back soon and take care. Don't disappear for too long!" In Norwegian: "Ta vare på deg selv, og ikke kom ut for uhell".

Vaffelkak/Rutatkak - In English: "A Norwegian waffle". In Norwegian: "Vaffel".

Matinnj & Sopinn - Both refer to the same meaning: "Hungry". In Norwegian: "Sulten".

Læven - "Noisy". In Norwegian: "Støy".

Åkkår - In English: "When you are too shy to help yourself twice with food!" In Norwegian: "Når du er for beskjeden".

Læms - In Norwegian: "Lefse". (A Norwegian traditional flatbread, resembling a tortilla, but sweeter, often with butter, sugar and cinnamon).

Brisen - "Tipsy". (Slightly drunk). In Norwegian: "Full".

Sjitat/Lortatt - "Dirty". In Norwegian: "skitten".

Gra - Unique word for Trøndere. "Horny". In Norwegian: "Kåt".

Høkkert - A redneck, but not always in a negative way. In Norwegian: "En slubbert" / "Harry person".

Suffisanse - In Norwegian: "Selvgodhet"/ "Selvsikkerhet". In English: "Self-righteousness" or "self-satisfaction".

Toillbaill - In Norwegian: "Tulling". In English: "crazy bastard" or "mad fool" It roughly translates to or in English, combining the word for crazy "toill" with a more aggressive, often derogatory word for a man "baill". It's typically used to describe someone in a reckless or foolish manner, with an emphasis on how out of control or absurd their actions are.

Itj - In Norwegian: "Ikke". In English: "Don't".

Læll - In Norwegian: "Likevel". In English: "Nevertheless".

Læn - In Norwegian: "Morsomt". In English: "Funny".

Snavvel - In Norwegian: "Godteri". In English: "Candy".

Disse - In Norwegian: "Huske" for barn. In English: "A swing set for children".

Karsk - "Coffee with strong liquor" (home brewed),

Heimert - In Norwegian: "Hjemmebrent". In English: "moonshine or home brewed, strong liquor".

Gæli - In Norwegian: "Galt". In English: "Wrong". - Sometimes referred to as a funny statement!

Sjø - In Norwegian: "Skjønner du?". In English: "Do you get it? Understand? Or amplifying if you really understand something".

Fotlaus - Literally translated: "A loose foot". Or "Drunk". In Norwegian: "Full".

Ful - In Norwegian: "Sint". In English: "Angry".

Kakskiv - In Norwegian: "Brødskive". In English: "Slice of bread with some sort of spread".

Hæ?! – In Norwegian: "Hva". In English: This is a typical Trøndersk expression, meaning "What?" or "Excuse me?". It's often said with a slight emphasis and a raised tone, reflecting the relaxed and some-what playful attitude of the region.

E' du heilt go i hue? - In Norwegian: "Er du helt god?". This phrase means: "Are you completely out of your mind?" It's often used in a lighthearted way, making it both an expression of surprise and good-natured humor.

Skinnkaldt – In Norwegian: "Iskaldt" - Literally translating to "skin cold", this term describes the biting, crisp cold that is common in Trondheim winters. It can refer to both the weather or the sensation of feeling cold, especially on your skin.

Ka e' dær? - In Norwegian: "Hva er dette?". This is a playful way of asking, "What's that?" and reflects the Trønders' relaxed style of questioning things.

Bæst – This is a Trøndersk twist on the word "best", and can be used in a variety of contexts, such as: "He's the best!"

Kaffi – A classic example of how Trøndersk adapts standard Norwegian. Instead of the usual: "kaffe", Trønders often say "kaffi".

Litjmuskveill - In Norwegian: "onsdag". In English: "Wednesday".

Gjørra – A variant of: "å gjøre" meaning "to do". In Trøndersk, it can often be used in a colloquial, laid-back context: "Skal vi gjørra det i morgen?" (Shall we do it tomorrow?).

Lættis – Meaning "funny" or "hilarious", this is a common word used in Trøndersk to describe something amusing. It's often said in a light-hearted, humorous context.

Noen æ – A variation of "noen av dere" (some of you), used informally in conversation: Har du snakka med noen æ? (Have you talked to any of them?).

Førr eit vær! – This phrase is used to express amazement or surprise at something or someone, often with a tone of incredulity: "Førr ei vær, det var imponerende!" (What a sight, that was impressive!).

Bæss – Another term meaning "best", commonly used when you want to emphasize something as excellent or top-notch. For example, "Han e' bæss på ski!" (He's the best at skiing!).

Ærli – Meaning "really", this is a strong emphasis, like saying "seriously" or "for real" in English. "Det va' ærli gøy" (It was really fun).

Gå i væggen – A funny Trøndersk expression meaning: "to hit the wall" or to be overwhelmed by something. It's used when something is too much or when you've reached your limit. Example: "Æ må gå i veggen!" (I need a break, I'm overwhelmed!).

Heim – In Norwegian: "hjem". Trøndersk uses "heim". For example, "Æ ska heim" means "I'm going home. It's a simple but recognizable feature of the dialect.

Tæ'n – In Norwegian: "De"/ "dem". Trønders often use "tæ'n" instead of "they". For instance, "Tæ'r har gått tur" means "They've gone for a walk". It's a bit of an endearing, informal twist on standard Norwegian.

Bærre lækkert – Used to describe something that's "really good" or "tasty" often in reference to food. You might hear it after a delicious meal: "Det va' bærre lækkert!" (That was really good!).

Æ skjønna itj – This is a very Trøndersk way of saying "I don't understand". The pronunciation is more relaxed compared to standard Norwegian: "Jeg skjønner ikke hva du mener". (I don't understand what you mean.)

Sei itj dær! – In Norwegian: "Ikke si det der".Translates to "Don't say that!". It's often used in a playful or teasing way. Example: "Sei itj dær, det e jo på ekte!" (Don't say that, it's really happening!).

Nu e' det no'n skjære! – A classic Trøndersk way of saying: "Now, there's something serious going on!" It's often used when something unexpected or exciting is happening. "Nu e' det no'n skjære på skolen!" (Now something's really happening at school!).

Skrøp – In Norwegian: "Skrøpelig". This is a playful way to describe someone or something as weak or fragile. You could use it for a person who's feeling under the weather or for an object that's falling apart. "Han e' litt skrøp i dag" (He's a bit weak today).

Kjapp i køen – Literally means "quick in the line", but it's used to describe someone who's impatient or always in a rush. "Du e' kjapp i køen!" (You're always in a hurry!).

Rykte som en oxe – Used to describe someone who is working hard or putting in a lot of effort, similar to saying "work like a horse" in English. Example: "Han rykte som en oxe på jobben!" (He's working hard like a horse at work!).

Han e' sjæfen – A casual way of saying "He's the boss", often used affectionately or with a little humor. "Han e' sjefen når det gjelder ski!" (He's the boss when it comes to skiing!).

Bjønnsliten – In Norwegian: "Kjempe sliten!". In Trøndersk this is a classic phrase meaning "dead tired" or "exhausted" often used to describe someone who has had a very long day. "Æ e' bjønnsliten etter jobben!" (I'm dead tired after work!).

Sprett på'n – In Norwegian: "Kom igjen"/ "fort deg". This means "let's go!" or "get moving!" It's an expression used to encourage someone to get started or hurry up. "Sprett på'n, vi skal rekke toget!" (Let's go, we need to catch the train!).

Skjærp dæ! – This phrase means "Get your act together!" or "Pull yourself together!" It's a friendly way to tell someone to focus or stop being silly. "Skjærp dæ, vi har mye å gjøre!" (Pull yourself together, we have a lot to do!).

Hæng med! – A way of saying "Stay with it!" or "Keep up!" It's often used when someone is lagging behind or not following along: "Heng med på praten!" (Keep up with the conversation!).

Rett på sak – A direct way of saying "Let's get to the point!" or "Straight to the point!" This is a very Trøndersk way of cutting to the chase in a conversation. "Rett på sak, hva vil du?" (Straight to the point, what do you want?).

Tøft som faen – A more intense expression, meaning "tough as hell". It's used to describe something or someone that's really tough, either in an impressive or difficult sense. "Den turen va' tøft som faen!" (That hike was tough as hell!).

Æ ska itj klag – Meaning "I won't complain" often used to express satisfaction or to convey that things are okay. "Æ ska itj klage, det e' fint her!" (I won't complain, it's nice here!).

Gå rundt grøten – This means "beat around the bush", and it's used when someone isn't getting to the point. "Slutt å gå rundt grøten, si hva du mener!" (Stop beating around the bush, say what you mean!).

Det e' som å trekke torsk på land – A quirky expression meaning "It's like pulling a fish onto land". It's used when something is awkward or unnatural. Example: "Det e' som å trekke torsk på land å prøve å forklare det". (It's like pulling a fish onto land trying to explain that).

Skjær dæ ut – This is a casual phrase used to tell someone to "cut it out" or "knock it off". Often used when someone is doing something a bit annoying: "Skjær dæ ut, det e' nok no!" (Cut it out, that's enough!).

Ska æ se på det? – A common way of saying "Should I look at it?" or "Do you want me to take a look?" Often used when someone is asking for help or offering assistance: "Ska æ se på det, eller klarer du det?" (Should I look at it, or can you handle it?).

Du e' heilt på bærtur – A funny expression meaning "You're completely off track" or "You're lost." It's used when someone is way off with their thoughts or actions: "Du e' helt på bærtur hvis du tenker sånn!" (You're completely off track if you think like that!).

Hælt på vits – In Norwegian: "Du tuller!" A playful phrase used to describe someone who's joking or being sarcastic. It's akin to saying "Just kidding" or "Pulling your leg".

For example, "Du e' hælt på vits når du sier at du har sett et troll!" (You're totally kidding when you say you saw a troll!).

Få dæ på'n – In Norwegian: "Få dæ på'n, vi skal gå!" (Get to it, we're leaving!).This means "Get to it" or "Start doing something", often used when someone is procrastinating or being slow.

Tørr i maska – In Norwegian: "Han e' tørr i maska når han prate om politikk!" (He's got a serious face when he talks about politics!). An expression meaning "serious face" or "stone-faced." It can be used when someone is trying to be serious or acting very serious.

Skrubb! – In Norwegian: "Skrubb, æ ska ha den siste øl'n!" (Scram, I'm having the last beer!). A fun way to tell someone to "get lost" or "scram." It's playful and not meant to be too harsh.

E' du snill å fjæsl – In Norwegian: "Slutt å tulle". A classic way of asking someone to "stop messing around" or "don't play games". It's often used when someone's being playful or too cheeky: "E' du snill å fjæsl, det e' viktig!" (Can you stop playing around, this is important!).

Bæsseling – In Norwegian: "Æ e' litt bæsseling (problemer) med å finne nøklene". (I'm having a bit of trouble finding my keys). A Trøndersk term for a small mess or a bit of trouble. It's the kind of word you'd use when things aren't quite going smoothly.

Kjøss på'n! – In Norwegian: "Vi ska gå ut og ta en kjøss på'n!" (We're going out to have a blast!). An expression used when something is going really well or someone is in a good mood. It's like saying "Kiss it!" in an exciting, fun way.

De er null stress – An easygoing way of saying "It's no problem" or "Don't worry about it". "Du kan ringe meg senere, det e' null stress". (You can call me later, it's no problem!).

Gå å lægg dæ! – Used to tell someone to "Go to bed!" or "Stop being silly!" It's an affectionate way to tell someone to rest. "Æ e' bjønnsliten, gå å legg dæ!" (I'm dead tired, go to bed!).

Bøggen - In Norwegian: "Politi" – "Police".

Fett-tjuv - In Norwegian: "Casanova"/ "sjarmør" – "A casanova".

Ganklæbb - In Norwegian: "Brunost" – "Brown cheese".

Gauder - In Norwegian: "Idiot" – "An idiot".

Hossolæsta - In Norwegian: "Ullsokker" – "Woolen socks".

Karravolin - In Norwegian: "Å yppe" – "To tease"/ "To provoke".

Kurinj - In Norwegian: "Dårlig"/ "fyllesjuk" (Another word with same meaning: foilljsjuk) – "Hangover".

Veitj/kveite/tæv/taus - In Norwegian: "Jente" – "Girl".

Ørtævv - In Norwegian: "Ørefik" – "A smack on the ear".

Sjøla/Sjøli`n - In Norwegian: "Mamma"/ "Pappa" – "Mum" or "Dad".

Kop - In Norwegian: "Treiging" – "Slowpoke" or "Sluggish".

Jæfs i låt, au au - In Norwegian: "Når du skader deg". In English: "When you get hurt!"

Toillkuk - In Norwegian: En skøyer eller idiot, kommer an på tonefallet – "crazy dick" is a very vulgar and offensive slang term in Norwegian, often used in a derogatory or aggressive manner. It literally translates to in English, combining a slang word for "crazy" or "insane" with a crude term for male genitalia. It's used to insult someone, typically implying that the person is foolish, reckless, or out of control in a negative way.

Spainnhøvv/Superkålhøvv - In Norwegian: "Idiot" – "An idiot".

Blængdall - is a very informal slang from the Trøndersk dialect, typically used to describe someone who is being a fool or acting recklessly. The term is often used in a playful or teasing manner, referring to a person who's being silly, foolish, or out of control in some way. It's similar to calling someone a "joker" or a "clown" in English, but with a more regional flair, often used with some affection rather than pure insult. In Norwegian: "En tulling".

Kjærringjækel - In Norwegian: "Djevelkjærring". In Enligsh: "A devil woman"/ "she-devil": is a Norwegian term, which it roughly translates to or in English. It is a highly derogatory and offensive phrase used to describe a woman who is seen as wicked, difficult, or unpleasant, often implying she is manipulative or malicious. The term combines "djevel" (devil) and "kjærring" (an old-fashioned word for woman or wife, often with a negative or dismissive connotation).

Brækkækkel - In Norwegian: "En som er så ekkel at man blir kvalm og spyr". Trøn-derskclumsy or awkward person: "breakneck" or "klutz"is a term from the dialect and is used to describe or refer to someone who is prone to accidents, particularly physical ones, like tripping or dropping things.

Daill - In Norwegian: "Tull", "småpirk" – "nonsense", "rubbish" or "silly".

Flørr'æ - In Norwegian: "Flytt deg" – "Move"/ "Move over".

Gakkorikaill - In Norwegian: "Spøkefull" – "Playful" or "Joking" or in English. It refers to someone who is lighthearted, teasing, or humorous, often in a way that is intended to entertain or amuse others.

Jabbkråk - In Norwegian: "Skravlekjerring" – "Gossiper" or "chatterbox", but referred to females only.

Toillat – In Norwegian: Er et uformelt, trøndersk uttrykk som ofte brukes for å beskrive noe som er skikkelig bra, imponerende, eller til og med overdrevent bra - som å gi uttrykk for at noe er "helt konge" eller "helt fantastisk". In English: "Totally awesome".

Gjetord – In Norwegian: Brukes ofte for å beskrive en form for underdrivelse eller noe som virker usannsynlig eller utrolig! In English: similar to saying "a far-fetched claim" or "an unbelievable story".

Fønvind – In Norwegian: En type vind eller brukt metaforisk for å beskrive noe som skjer plutselig og uventet. In English: A type of wind, or used metaphorically to describe something that happens suddenly and unexpectedly.

Snedig – In Norwegian: "smart", "lurt" og "morsomt". In English: "Funny", "smart".

E det moli? – In Norwegian: "Er det mulig?" "Seriøst?" "Går det an?". In English: "Are you for real?"

Æ is pronounced: (Similar to the letter a in cat)

E is pronounced: (As E in name Elle)

I is pronounced: (As the English letter E)

A is pronounced: (As the English word 'father')

Å is pronounced: (As the English word 'Law' or 'Awe')

Ø is pronounced: (Somewhat like the English word 'Hurt')

Æ E I A Æ Å – Is actually a sentence in Trøndersk – believe it or not!
In Bokmål, (the official Norwegian language) it is translated to: "Jeg
går i a jeg også". Which again in English is translated to: "I am in
class A too". (The classes in the Norwegian school system are often
divided into letters from the alphabet.)

The Trønders truly love talking in vowels alone!

"When a Trønder says "It's fine," it often means:
"Get ready for an adventure."

–T

Social Interactions and Relationships

Dating a Trønder

Socializing with Trøndere is like joining an exclusive club where the password is "hygge," but you also need to be able to handle awkward silences and the occasional deadpan humor. They'll invite you into their home, offer you coffee, and probably give you a lecture on why *koldtbord* (a traditional Scandinavian buffet-style meal with cold cuts and cheese and pickled herrings etc.) is the best meal, but don't expect a lot of small talk. The art of a Trønder conversation? Start with a "How are you?" and then immediately dive into a discussion about the weather, local politics, or which fjord is the most "authentic," And if you're lucky, they might even crack a smile. Just remember: when a Trønder says "it's fine," it usually means "prepare for an adventure!"

1. The 'Nordic Nod': When Silence Speaks Louder Than Words

Trøndere are masters of the silent acknowledgment, the infamous Nordic Nod. You pass a fellow Trønder on the street, exchange a quick glance, and the nod seals the deal. It's simple, effective, and yet, hilarious when tourists try to mimic it and end up giving a full-on head bob like they're doing a slow dance.

Funny Take:

Tourist: "I tried to be friendly with a Trønder nod. Ended up looking like I was in a cabbage-picking competition."

2. Asking for Directions: A Lesson in Trøndersk Precision

Ask a Trønder for directions, and you'll a firm 'ja', 'næi', 'veit itj, sorry', or you could end up getting more detail than you bargained for. Especially in the more rural Trøndelag. What might have been a simple "turn left" turns into a 10-minute explanation involving fjords, trolls, and whether or not you should bring a fishing rod for the journey!

3. The Classic 'What Do You Mean?' Conversation

Trøndere aren't ones to sugarcoat their opinions, and that's part of what makes social interactions so entertaining. Whether it's a comment on the weather, local politics, or a simple question about food, you're guaranteed a dry, witty response.

Funny Take:
Stranger: "It's a bit chilly today, don't you think?"
Trønder: "Jau, men det blir likar". (Yes, but it will get better.)

4. Tourist Orders: When the Menu is a Challenge

Tourists often underestimate the complexities of a Trøndersk menu. Whether it's figuring out what rakfisk actually is or understanding the difference between *klubb* and *læms*, social interactions can get hilariously awkward when someone attempts to order something "Norwegian."

Funny Take:
Tourist: "I'll have the fish dish."
Waiter: "Lutefisk, bacalao, or simply fiskeboller?"
Tourist: "Wait, are these all fish dishes?"

5. The Friendly Debate: Trøndersk vs. The Rest of Norway

You know you're having a good time when a casual conversation turns into a full-on debate about which region is better. Trøndelag or the rest of Norway. Whether it's a festival, dialect differences, or just bragging rights over the best skiing spots, it's always fun (and a bit competitive) to see Trøndere defend their home turf.

Funny Take:

Trønder Friend: "Oslo? Yeah, it's nice for tourists. But for real charm, come to Trondheim. We've got the fjords and fewer traffic jams."
Stranger: "Isn't it colder here?"
Trønder: "Colder? Sure. But we've got more humor to keep us warm."

6. The Silent Treatment: When You're Still in the Wrong

Trøndere have perfected the art of the silent treatment, especially in cases where tourists or newcomers make a social faux pas. Whether it's missing the right social cue or giving unsolicited advice, you'll find yourself on the receiving end of a few raised eyebrows and deadpan stares.

Funny Take:
Stranger: "I don't think this café needs reservations."
Trønder: Silent nod, followed by a 'see you later when you're hungry' look.

Funny Anecdotes of Dating a Trønder

Dating a Trønder comes with its fair share of quirks, humor, and unique cultural experiences. From navigating their blunt honesty to trying to keep up with their love for traditional foods and practical jokes, dating a Trønder adds an adventurous twist to relationships. Here are some amusing anecdotes that capture the charm and humor of social interactions with Trønder men.

1. The "Short Answers" Saga

One of the first things newcomers to Trøndelag notice is how direct Trøndere can be, especially when it comes to conversation. You might ask a simple question like, "Do you want to go out for dinner?" and receive a straightforward answer:
Trønder Man: "Ja."
That's it. Just "Ja." No extra details, no elaboration. It's part of the local charm, but when you first experience it, you might find yourself wondering if he's interested or not. Eventually, you learn to read between the lines, or simply accept that Trøndere aren't big on small talk.

2. The "Practical Date" Night

One humorous aspect of dating a Trønder is how they approach dates with a certain practicality. Whether it's a first date or an anniversary dinner, expect moments where efficiency reigns supreme. Instead of a long, drawn-out dinner, a Trønder might suggest something like:

"We could grab a burger or a frozen pizza, and then go for a walk on the quay."

While other regions might plan grand dinner dates with wine and candles, Trøndere prefer something simpler, but somehow, it always turns out to be memorable.

3. The "Troll Tour" Test

If you're dating a Trønder, be prepared for some whimsical, yet slightly odd, experiences involving local legends and traditions. One particular fun challenge is being introduced to the world of trolls, literally. On your first visit to a nearby forest or mountain hike, your Trønder partner might give you a "crash course" on every troll tale in the area. You'll hear everything from how trolls freeze in sunlight to how they like to play tricks on hikers. Best to just nod and smile; otherwise, they'll keep going all day!

4. The "Fishing Expedition" Date

Fishing is a big part of Trønder culture, so expect a few surprises if you're out on a fishing trip with a Trønder man. They'll likely have a keen eye on how many fish you're catching, but don't expect praise for your catch, it's all about whether it's big enough and if it was caught "the right way." If you catch a fish that doesn't meet their standards, you'll hear phrases like:

"Eh, not bad... for a beginner."

It's all in good fun, but after a while, you'll start wondering if you've been inducted into the unofficial "Fishing Hall of Fame."

Dating a Trønder man means embracing a lifestyle filled with humor, tradition, and a touch of practicality. Their close-knit community values and love for local quirks create moments of genuine connection and laughter. Whether you're hiking through forests filled with trolls or navigating the practicalities of everyday life, being part of a Trønder's world is an experience that leaves you with unforgettable stories, and a healthy sense of humor.

Here are some tips on how to navigate dating a Trønder man:

1. Appreciate Their Directness

Trøndere are famously blunt and straightforward. When dating a Trønder, expect honest communication with little room for ambiguity. If you ask for an opinion, you'll get it, sometimes whether you want it or not! Embrace this trait and appreciate the clarity it brings.

Tip: Don't take offense if they give you a simple "Ja" or "Nei" (yes or no). They mean it, and respect is often expressed through clear, unfiltered answers.

2. Be Ready for Practical Dates

Trøndere tend to lean towards practicality when it comes to spending time together. Don't expect grand, elaborate dates. Instead, you might find yourselves enjoying a walk along the fjord, a fishing trip, or a good home cooked meal. These are the moments that Trøndere cherish, blending simplicity with deep connections.

Tip: Embrace these simple outings, they're often where the most memorable and meaningful conversations happen.

3. Laugh at Their Humor

Trøndere have a great sense of humor, often involving playful teasing, self-deprecation, and witty banter. They enjoy light-hearted humor, often with a touch of local folklore or regional jokes. Don't be surprised if trolls, fishing mishaps, or harsh winters are recurring topics.

Tip: Laugh with them, even if you don't get all the local references at first. Over time, you'll understand their unique brand of humor and enjoy the playful nature of conversations.

4. Be Patient with Their Independence

Trøndere are fiercely independent. They value their space and may not always express emotions in a way you're used to. This doesn't mean they don't care, it just means they show it differently. Over time, you'll notice small, thoughtful gestures of affection that reflect their care and loyalty.

Tip: Allow them the space they need, and in return, they'll show up for you in ways that are genuine and meaningful.

5. Learn to Navigate Their Love for Tradition

Trøndere have strong ties to their regional culture and traditions, from local foods like rakfisk to traditional music and festivals. Embrace these elements, even if they seem quirky at first. They'll appreciate your openness to their roots.

Tip: Join them in local celebrations and embrace the customs, there's always room for fun, even in the most traditional settings.

6. Expect Conversations About the Weather

Weather is a serious topic for Trøndere. Whether it's discussing the impending storm or the nuances of seasonal shifts, weather updates are a regular conversation. Embrace the meteorological chatter and find ways to turn it into playful banter.

Tip: Respond with humor or counter with your own weather predictions. It'll add an element of surprise to the conversation!

7. Support Their Community Ties

Trøndere value their community deeply. They're often surrounded by family, friends, and a strong local network. When dating a Trønder, it's important to appreciate these relationships and be open to spending time with their close-knit circle.

Tip: Participate in local gatherings and activities, they'll love that you're integrating into their world.

8. Stay Open to New Experiences

Dating a Trønder often comes with unexpected adventures. Whether it's a spontaneous road trip to a remote fjord or a visit to a historical site, be ready for surprises. Trøndere love experiences that connect them to nature, history, and their heritage.

Tip: Embrace these unique moments with enthusiasm, you'll create lasting memories.

9. Show Appreciation for Their Practical Side

Trøndere are pragmatic and prefer solutions over drama. They thrive in practical problem-solving, whether it's managing everyday challenges or navigating deeper emotional discussions. Appreciating this trait will earn you respect and strengthen your bond.

Tip: Engage in conversations that value logical reasoning, and watch how quickly trust is built.

10. A Sense of Adventure with a Touch of Practicality

Trøndere are lovers of adventure but always grounded in practicality. From suggesting spontaneous road trips to helping you navigate the rugged terrain, they'll make sure you feel safe while enjoying new experiences.

Example:

Trønder Man: "We could drive to that cabin with no plumbing nor electricity, (no need for fancy hotels). There's a cozy little place, and the stars look clearer out there."

Dating a Trønder man is a unique experience, especially when they're trying to impress a foreign woman. With their distinctive charm, down-to-earth approach, and a touch of local tradition, a Trønder man knows how to create memorable moments.

Freudian Slips:

Trønder: "Når kjæm du?"   (Translation: When are you coming? Bokmål Norwegian: Når kommer du?)

You: "Når kæm du?"

Trønder: Blank stare

'Skal': The Universal Verb That's Suddenly Confusing

"Skal" or also pronouced 'ska' (will) is a powerful verb in Trøndersk, but once you cross into northern Trøndelag, it takes on a whole new life. Instead of just skal, you'll hear ska or skæl.

Adding 'Hæ' and 'Ka' to Everything: The Trøndersk Question Mark
Once you've crossed into northern Trøndelag, hæ becomes a question mark in itself. Almost every statement ends with it, whether you know what you're asking or not. It's a whole new world of confusion.

Getting 'Æ' and 'Å' Mixed Up
Trøndersk thrives on Æ and Å. Southern Trøndelag makes it simple, but the further north you go, the more æ and å become indistinguishable until one day you're confidently asking for a båb instead of a bær.

So you've been dating a Trønder for a while, thought you had the dialect down. You've mastered the southern version of kaffe, skål, and hæl, and things were going smoothly... until you moved north. Suddenly, a whole new language emerges, and your in-laws sound like they've stepped straight out of a dialect comedy sketch. Dialect Jumps, when you realize you're entirely lost. You thought you had the dialect covered, but no. One moment you're fine, and the next, your in-laws are speaking a new dialect that feels like learning an entirely different language.

Deadpan Family Reactions: Dialect Faux Pas
In-laws have mastered the art of the deadpan reactions. Whether you slip up in pronunciation or say something unintentionally hilarious, they'll respond with a look so flat, it's practically a full-on comedy sketch, leaving you to feel slightly uncomfortable and a tad confused.

Conclusion

Dating and socializing with a Trønder means embracing a world where dialects evolve every kilometer, and Freudian slips are the norm. From confusing vowels to masterfully crafted deadpan responses, every social interaction is a comedy show waiting to happen. And somehow, that's what makes it all so wonderfully entertaining!

Food and Traditions

Why go to France for cheese and charcuterie when the Trønders have mastered it?! We have Grilstad factory, founded in Trondheim in 1957, serving cured meats, sausages and other deli products. Grilstad is a leading producer in Norway, where you can enjoy world class meats, local cheeses, flatbread and more. Charcuterie with a Norwegian twist! Inderøya, in Trøndelag has been recognized for its exceptional food products. In October 2023, Gangstad Gårdsysteri, a dairy farm located in Inderøy, won the prestigious World Cheese Awards with their blue cheese, *Nidelven Blå*. This cheese was selected as the world's best among 4,502 entries from 43 countries.

At *Nidar Bergene,* you can taste world-class chocolate in its own right, with unique nordic flavors and high quality ingredients. The Trøndersk chocolate factory founded in 1912 in Trondheim is a perfect mix of Trøndersk delicious chocolate and Norwegian nostalgia. While it may not have the same international reputation as swiss or belgium chocolate. Nidar holds a special place in Norwegian hearts. The *melkesjokolade* has quite the reputation abroad. Having been savored by many Americans, Australians, and others who have had the chance to try it, either through travel to Norway, Norwegian friends, or imported goods, find it irresistibly delightful.

Its distinctive taste is often attributed to the high-quality Norwegian milk and traditional recipes used in production. Travelers and expatriates frequently stock up on Melkesjokolade to bring home, and it has earned a reputation as a coveted souvenir.

Have you noticed how it compares to other milk chocolates abroad?

Trøndelag has a rich tradition of producing world-class food and beverages, with several local products receiving prestigious awards in recent years.

Beer Achievements

E.C. Dahls Brewery: In 2023, their flagship **Dahls Pils** was awarded gold in the "International Style Lager" category at the European Beer Star Awards, Europe's most prestigious beer competition.

Kong Vinter: This dark bock beer from E.C. Dahls Brewery won gold in the "German Style Dunkler Bock" category at the European Beer Star Awards in 2021.

At the **Trøndelag Food Festival**, an annual event celebrating the region's culinary excellence, several local products have been recognized:

Best Baked Good and Grain Product: *Italian Brioche* by Stokkøy Bakeri.

Best Meat Product: *Pinnekjøtt of Cashmere Goat* by Elset Gård.

Best Dairy Product: *Norwegian Stracciatella* by Toddum Gårdsysteri.

Best Seafood Product: *Rakfisk of Blåfjellrøye* by LiVERTEN AS.

Best Sweet Treat: *Smaksbomber (Flavorbombs) Salty Caramel* by Fru Nelik.

Best Newcomer: *FrostaChips, Dill Pickle* by FrostaChips.

Best Organic Product: *Grotteost* by Hitra Gårdsmat.

Best Food Gift: *Ølsmaking (Beer Tasting)* by Smaker fra Øyriket.

Best Drink: *VI Aquavit* by Inderøy Brenneri.

No discussion about Trøndersk cuisine would be complete without mentioning some of its iconic traditional dishes:

Sodd

A classic Trøndersk dish that holds a special place in the hearts of the locals. It's a traditional soup made with:

Meat: Typically lamb or mutton, boiled until tender.

Meatballs: Small, flavorful meatballs often made from a mix of lamb and beef.

Vegetables: Potatoes and carrots are boiled alongside the meat.

Sodd is a staple at celebrations like weddings, baptisms, and confirmations, or even funerals, often served with flatbrød (flatbread).

Klubb (or Raspeballer)

Also known as "potetball" in other regions, klubb is a hearty and filling potato dumpling dish:

Ingredients: Made from grated raw potatoes mixed with flour, sometimes with a cube of salted pork fat hidden inside.

Served With: Typically enjoyed with salted pork, bacon, or lamb, and a side of melted butter or syrup.

Klubb **is the perfect comfort food for cold Trøndelag evenings, representing the resourcefulness of traditional Nordic cuisine.**

Other noteworthy traditional dishes

Lefse: A soft flatbread often served as a dessert, spread with butter and sugar.

Rakfisk: Fermented fish, often an acquired taste but a beloved delicacy for locals.

Fårikål: While not exclusive to Trøndelag, this mutton and cabbage stew is a Norwegian favorite during the fall.

"Forget the Grandiosa culture, forget the lutefisk nightmares; this is a city with Michelin-starred restaurants, Nordic fusion dishes that look like edible art, and seafood so fresh it probably swam here faster than your boat."

– T

TRONDHEIM THROUGH THE AGES - THE HISTORICAL HEART OF NORWAY

Trondheim has a rich and significant history, which has shaped the culture of its people, the Trøndere.

Trondheim, founded in 997 AD by Viking King Olav Tryggvason, is more than just a scenic city with colorful wooden houses, it's a city with a deep-rooted place in Norway's history. Once known as Nidaros, it was the nation's first capital and an important religious, cultural, and political hub during the Viking and medieval periods.

The Founding of Nidaros

In the late 10th century, Olav Tryggvason chose the site at the mouth of the Nidelva River to establish a new trading post and fort. Surrounded by water on three sides, Trondheim's location made it a natural center for trade and travel, allowing it to flourish early on. It quickly became a seat of power, both for the Viking rulers and later, the Christian kings.

The Rise of St. Olav

One of Trondheim's most significant historical figures is King Olav II Haraldsson, later known as St. Olav. After dying in the Battle of Stiklestad in 1030, Olav was canonized as a saint, and his shrine became a major pilgrimage site in Trondheim. The Nidaros

Cathedral, built in his honor, remains one of the most iconic landmarks in the city and continues to be a central point of Norwegian religious and historical identity.

Nidaros Cathedral – A Symbol of Norwegian Unity

Nidaros Cathedral is the most important Gothic structure in Norway and has been the coronation site for Norwegian kings for centuries. The cathedral not only reflects Trondheim's significance as a religious center during the Middle Ages but also serves as a unifying symbol for the Norwegian people. Pilgrims still walk the historic "Olav's Way" (Olavsveien) to visit the cathedral and pay homage to St. Olav, linking modern Trondheim to its medieval roots.

THE CITY THAT ROSE (AND BURNED, AND ROSE AGAIN)

Trondheim's history reads a bit like a soap opera: founded by a Viking, blessed by a saint, burned to the ground (multiple times), and yet, like any good drama queen, it always comes back looking better than before.

(Or does it? debatable, I suppose, but that's an entirely different book!)

The Viking with Big Plans

It all started with Olav Tryggvason, a Viking king who thought, "Hey, this spot by the river would make a great city." So, he founded Nidaros (because why not name it something cool and mysterious?). Little did Olav know that this would eventually become a city famous for its breathtaking cathedrals, and for repeatedly catching on fire. But hey, nothing worth having comes easy, right?

St. Olav – The Saint Who Refused to Stay Dead

Speaking of drama, let's not forget King Olav II Haraldsson. After dying in the Battle of Stiklestad, he decided that death wasn't enough of a legacy and came back as a saint. His shrine in Nidaros Cathedral became the place to be in medieval Norway, attracting pilgrims like it was some kind of medieval Coachella. Forget selfies, back then, it was all about lighting candles for St. Olav and hoping he'd put in a good word for you upstairs.

The Vikings and Trønders – Horned Helmets and Hytte Dreams

If you think the Trøndere are chill, you haven't met their Viking ancestors. These guys were the original overachievers: sailing off to conquer new lands one day, farming potatoes the next. Trønders back in the Viking days were just as comfortable raiding monasteries as they were discussing the best way to grow turnips. You know, balance.

Viking Power and Fashion Statements
Forget what Hollywood tells you. Vikings didn't wear horned helmets. But Trønders did have a flair for the dramatic. They were the Viking version of multitaskers, running a farm during the day and going off on the odd raid at night. Some even argue that their love for practical fashion (think cozy wool) has stuck around, which might explain why modern-day Trønders are obsessed with hiking gear.

The Original Democracy: Frostatinget
In between all that pillaging, the Trøndere decided they should also be civilized. Enter Frostatinget, an early version of Norway's parliament, where Viking chieftains came together to discuss laws, settle disputes, and, probably argue about who had the best beard. It was democracy, Viking-style: serious debates, followed by a feast and maybe a bit of brawling for good measure.

How the Trøndere Were Christianized (Against Their Will)
If there's one thing you don't want to do, it's tell a Trønder what to believe in. So when King Olav Tryggvason showed up in the 10th century with a new religion and a sword to match, the Trøndere were understandably skeptical. But, like any good Viking, Olav believed in persuasion through, well, force.

Olav Tryggvason – The Viking Missionary
King Olav didn't exactly go door-to-door with pamphlets and a smile. His version of converting the Trønders involved a lot more swords and a lot less subtlety. It was like convincing your stubborn uncle to switch his favorite football team, except with axes. Eventually, the Trøndere caved, but you can bet they still kept a few of their old gods on speed dial, just in case.

St. Olav – The Viking Turned Saint
Fast forward to St. Olav, who took things a step further by dying and becoming a saint.

Now, that's dedication. Trondheim soon became the Norwegian Vatican, complete with Nidaros Cathedral, where people came to pray, celebrate, and, let's be honest, probably gossip about whose Viking ancestor was tougher.

Fires, Kings, and Fishing – Trondheim's Medieval Glory (and Repeated Failures to Stay Fireproof)

You know you're important when the universe keeps trying to set you on fire and you just keep coming back stronger. Trondheim, as Norway's medieval powerhouse, was so full of action that it couldn't stop burning down. But like a phoenix (or just really determined Norwegians), the Trøndere rebuilt the city again and again—until someone finally figured out that wood buildings might not be the best idea.

Royal Crowns and Trading Herring

Trondheim was not only Norway's spiritual capital, but it was also the place to be if you wanted to trade, be crowned king, or just enjoy a good bowl of fish soup. Medieval Trondheim was the ultimate combination of royal glamour and fishy business deals. Sure, there was the occasional Viking raid, but the real action was in the marketplace, where Trøndere showed off their herring-trading skills like it was a competitive sport.

The Great Fires – AKA Trondheim's Favorite Pastime

Trondheim must have had some really bad luck, or an over-enthusiastic love for wooden houses, because it burned down several times. The Great Fire of 1681 was so epic that they had to redesign the entire city. And who do they call for help? A French guy named Cicignon, who gave Trondheim its modern street layout, proving that when in doubt, go European.

Trondheim Today – From Viking Raids to Tech Startups

These days, Trondheim is more about coding than conquering. Thanks to the Norwegian University of Science and Technology (NTNU), the city has traded in Viking longboats for laptops, becoming a hub for students, researchers, and tech startups. But don't worry, the Trønders still keep it real with their love of nature, coffee, and a good hytte weekend.

NTNU – Where Vikings Would Probably Be IT Professionals

Trondheim's NTNU has turned the city into Norway's brainiest hangout. Imagine a Viking, but instead of sailing off to pillage, he's coding the next big app and hiking on weekends. That's pretty much the vibe. And while the Trøndere have left their axes at home, they still love a challenge, only now, it's about solving problems in engineering and sustainability, and neuroscience.

Cabin Fever (But in a Good Way)

Despite all the tech, Trønders haven't lost touch with their roots. Weekends are still spent escaping to their beloved "hytte," where there's no Wi-Fi, but plenty of wood to chop and nature to enjoy. It's a far cry from the city's Viking days, but in some ways, nothing has changed. Trønders still know how to balance hard work with hard relaxation.

Myths, Tales and Legends

Trøndelag, including Trondheim and its surrounding areas, is rich with myths, tales, and legends that reflect the region's history, nature, and unique culture. Here are some notable ones:

1.Huldra (A Seductive Forrest Spirit)
The flirtatious temptress with alluring songs and enchanting beauty. You won't notice her cow tail before after you have been seduced by her.

2. Fossegrimen (The Water Spirit)
Legend: The Fossegrimen is a mystical water spirit that inhabits waterfalls and rivers in Trøndelag. It is known for luring humans by playing enchanting melodies by the water sometimes leading them to drown or disappear.

Humorous Twist: Trøndere are always wary of meeting a Fossegrimen, especially those who play music near the powerful waterfalls of Verdal or Selbu. They tend to keep a safe distance!

3. The Monk' Ghost
Nidaros Cathedral (Trondheim) is said to be haunted by a monk ghost. It is believed he was buried within the cathedral, and his spirit guards the ancient relics within.

4. The Trøndelag Giant
A giant named Gråkallen is said to roam the mountains of Trøndelag, watching over the

region and guarding hidden treasures. He's often depicted as both intimidating and wise.

Humorous Twist: Many Trøndere playfully compare local figures to Gråkallen, claiming they have his size and wisdom when discussing tough problems!

5. Trollheimen and the Trolls

Trollheimen, the mountain range near Trondheim, is believed to be the home of trolls. These supernatural creatures come alive in the dark, causing mischief and sometimes transforming into humans during the day.

Humorous Twist: Trøndere enjoy telling stories of encounters with trolls, exaggerating their size, clumsiness, and inability to understand modern technology, like how they'd react to a smartphone!

6. Munkholmen and the Ghostly Monks

Munkholmen, the island fortress near Trondheim, is haunted by the ghosts of monks who were executed there during the Reformation. Visitors report strange noises and ghostly apparitions.

7. Nidelva and the River Serpent

The Nidelva River is said to house a serpent-like creature that rises from the depths during full moons. It is feared by fishermen and travelers, especially after a few local legends claim encounters with the elusive beast.

Humorous Twist: Some locals believe the serpent shows up during particularly heavy rain, blaming it for blocking fishing spots or stealing fish!

8. The Nidaros Cathedral Treasure

Nidaros Cathedral is said to house a hidden treasure buried beneath its foundations, protected by mystical forces. Stories circulate about adventurers who've searched for it, only to disappear mysteriously.

Humorous Twist: Modern legends suggest the treasure is merely forgotten casks of ancient beer, hidden away during medieval feasts, waiting to be uncovered by daring explorers!

These myths and legends not only enrich the cultural identity of Trøndelag but also add a layer of humor and storytelling that has been cherished by locals for generations.

9. The Spirit of Stiklestad Battlefield

Stiklestad is the site of Norway's most famous medieval battle. After the fierce conflict, the spirits of warriors are said to linger, fighting invisible skirmishes in the fields and forests.

10.The Mystery of the Steinkjer Stone Circle

A circle of ancient stones near Steinkjer is believed to be a gathering spot for spirits of ancient druids who practiced dark magic. Anyone who disrupts the stones will suffer bad luck.

11. The Ghost of Trondheim's Old Library

The old Trondheim Public Library, which dates back to the 19th century, is said to be haunted by the ghost of a librarian who loved books so much that they couldn't leave the shelves after death.

12. The Lake Monster of Oppdal

Lake Oppdal is rumored to hide a mysterious creature known as Oppdalsormen, resembling a serpent. Witnesses claim to see ripples and shadowy forms beneath the water.

Humorous Twist: In local folklore, Oppdalsormen is blamed whenever visitors catch nothing during a fishing trip "It's the serpent stealing the fish again!"

13. Hell, a small town in Trøndelag, (just next to the airport) is home to the Hell Firestone, said to curse those who touch it with bad luck. People avoid it to this day, fearing the stone's powers.

Trondheim Torg - Julemarked

THE TRØNDELAG BUCKET LIST – HOW TO SPEND YOUR TIME IN TRONDHEIM LIKE A TRUE TRØNDER

Trondheim might not be Norway's biggest city, but it's packed with history, culture, and unique experiences. Whether you're a tourist or Norwegian born and raised, there are a few things you absolutely have to check off your list. Some are grand, others are quirky, but all of them are essential to experiencing Trondheim's charm.   So grab your umbrella (it's probably going to rain) and start exploring!

1. Nidaros Cathedral – The Heart of Trondheim

If you visit Trondheim and don't see Nidarosdomen, were you even really here? This towering Gothic cathedral is the most famous landmark in town and the northernmost medieval cathedral in the world. Built over the tomb of Saint Olaf, Norway's patron saint, it's been a pilgrimage site for centuries. Inside, marvel at the intricate stained glass windows, climb the tower for an epic view of the city, and don't forget to explore the crypts below (if you're not afraid of ghosts from the 11th century).

Pro Tip: Visit during one of the majestic organ concerts to feel like you're in a Viking saga.

2. Bakklandet – Trondheim's Cozy, Colorful Quarter

Bakklandet is Trondheim's postcard-perfect neighborhood, with its narrow cobblestone streets, colorful wooden houses, and cozy cafes. It's the kind of place where you can wander for hours, sipping coffee and pretending you're in a Norwegian fairy tale. This is where you'll find Trondheim's famous bike lift (Trampe), the world's first and only lift designed for cyclists. Even if you don't cycle, watching someone brave the lift is always entertaining.

Must-do: Grab a cinnamon bun at Baklandet Skydsstation, (Which dates back to 1700 C) or their fish soup, and enjoy it while gazing out over the old town bridge (Gamle Bybro).

Trønders are definitely coffee lovers at heart, but tea does have a small, quiet place in their routine, especially when it comes to relaxing or feeling under the weather. So, if you're a tea drinker visiting Trondheim, you'll find options, but coffee is where the local passion truly lies! Whether you're looking for the perfect flat white, a cozy nook to escape the rain, or a spot to get some work done with a strong cup of black coffee, Trondheim's café scene has you covered. Enjoy your coffee crawl!

3. Kristiansten Fortress – Views and Viking Vibes

Kristiansten Fortress has guarded Trondheim since the 17th century, and while its days of fending off Swedish invasions are over, it now offers the best panoramic views of the city and the fjord. The fortress is also a reminder of Trondheim's more serious past during World War II, with a memorial honoring those who resisted Nazi occupation.

Bonus: After hiking up to the fortress, reward yourself with a picnic while enjoying the view. And don't worry, it's not as steep as it looks!

4. Munkholmen – The Island of Many Faces

Take a short boat ride out to Munkholmen, a small island with a lot of history. It's been a monastery, a Viking execution site, and a prison fortress. Now, it's a popular spot for a summer swim or a relaxed afternoon in the sun. You can tour the fortress or just sit by the water and soak up the view of Trondheim from the fjord.

Tip: On a sunny day, this is the perfect place to take a swim (but remember, this is Norway, so it'll be refreshing, to say the least!).

5. Rockheim – Norway's Museum of Pop and Rock Music

For music lovers, Rockheim is a must. Located in a futuristic building right by the harbor, this museum is dedicated to Norwegian pop and rock history. You'll find interactive exhibits on everyone from Åge Aleksandersen to A-ha, and even some pretty wild fashion choices from Norway's 1980s music scene. Whether you're into Trønderrock or Norwegian black metal, there's something for every music fan here.

Interactive Fun: Try your hand at mixing music in one of the sound studios, or test your karaoke skills with some classic Norwegian hits.

6. The Archbishop's Palace – Medieval Marvel

Right next to Nidaros Cathedral is the Archbishop's Palace, which houses the Crown Regalia (Norway's royal crowns and ceremonial gear). It's one of the oldest secular buildings in Scandinavia and offers an amazing glimpse into Norway's medieval past. This is also where Norwegian kings have been crowned since the Middle Ages, so you're walking in some seriously royal footsteps.

Must-see: The museum offers some fascinating exhibits on Trondheim's Viking and medieval history, so be sure to take a stroll through the past.

7. Sverresborg – Trøndelag's Open-Air Folk Museum

If you want to know what life was like for Trønders back in the day, head to Sverresborg, an open-air museum that features more than 80 historical buildings. From traditional farmhouses to an old-fashioned stave church, this place is a snapshot of Trøndelag's rural past. During summer, you'll even find actors dressed in traditional clothing, reenacting scenes from olden times.

For Families: There's also an exciting kids' area, with lots of activities that will keep young ones entertained while learning about history.

8. Lerkendal Stadium – The Holy Ground of Rosenborg Football

If you're a football fan, a visit to Lerkendal Stadium, home of Rosenborg BK, is non-negotiable. Rosenborg is Norway's most successful football club, and a visit to their stadium is like a pilgrimage for sports lovers. Whether it's game day or not, the atmosphere here is electric, and you can even take a tour of the stadium.

Pro Tip: If you're lucky enough to catch a match, join the local fans for an unforgettable experience, just make sure you know the words to "Vi e' stolt av å værra trønder" (We're proud to be Trønder) By Åge Aleksandersen!

9. Stiftsgården – The Royal Residence

Stiftsgården is the largest wooden palace in Scandinavia, and when the Norwegian royal family visits Trondheim, this is where they stay. Built in the late 18th century, it's an impressive example of Norwegian Baroque architecture. While it's not always open to the public, guided tours are available during the summer months, and even just admiring it from the outside is a treat.

Pro Tip: Keep an eye out during major Norwegian celebrations—this place becomes the focal point of royal parades and festivities.

10. Bymarka – The Great Outdoors Right Next Door

If you want to experience the true Trønder love of nature, head to Bymarka, a vast forested area with lakes, hiking trails, and skiing paths. Whether it's summer or winter, Bymarka is the perfect escape from the city. It's only a short bus or tram ride away, but you'll feel like you're deep in the wilderness. Trønders love to spend weekends here, hiking or cross-country skiing, depending on the season.

Tip: Bring a thermos of coffee and some waffles, you'll want a snack while taking in the view from one of the many lookout points.

11. **Lade** – Take a walk by the fjord from restpoint to restpoint and explore the beautiful views.

12. Visit The Botanical Gardens and Ringve Music Museum, both located in Lade.

13. Trondheim's vibrant art scene, with its numerous museums, galleries, and graffiti art walk tour, will add a fantastic cultural element to your stay. Just to name a few:

K.U.K
Trøndelag Museum

Hjorten Teater/ Posten Moderne (PoMo) – International Art Scene Gallery.

Trondheim kunstmuseum (art museum)

Kunsthall Trondheim (International Art Gallery.)

Trondheim Maritim Museum

Ringve Music Museum (music museum)

Sverresborg Folk Museum

Rockheim (rock music museum)

   The Jewish Museum of Trondheim

NTNU Vitenskapsmuseum (Science museum)

Vitensenteret (Science centre for kids and families.)

Justice Museum

Coastal Museum

Arch Bishops Museum

The Royal Regalia

Stiftsgården

Modern Art Gallery

   Dropsfabrikken

Galleri Ismene

Galleri SG

14. What about picnicking and kayaking on the river 'Nidelven'? The kayaks are rentable.

15. Go on a stroll and get to know all of trondhiem's districts. Solsiden for its many bars and restaurants. Svartlamon, the alternative district in Trondheim, and many more.

16. Take a 'mini' pilgrimage hike by taking the only remaining tram left in the city from Trondheim city centre to Lian. This leads on to a 7 km hike. Suitable for children as well as adults.

17. Tyholttårnet (A 124 meter tall radio tower) It has an observation desk, and a family friendly revolving restaurant, as awell as fantastic views over Trondhiem. A great place to see the full scale of the city.

18. Are you comfortable in the cold? What about ice bathing? Don't worry, at 'Havet Arena' there are saunas outdoors for your comfort to warm up again.

19.If you are visiting during December, don't miss the 'Julemarked'. The Nordics biggest and best Christmas market. With countless booths, music, and delicious treats.

Places outside of Trondheim and locals recommendations to other places in Trøndelag:

Hell   is

a place where you arrive when entering Trondheim via airplane. Close to the airport. Hell in Norwegian means something completely different then you think! In norsk it means luck and happiness. Many find it amusing to visit Hell and its 'Hollywood' sign on the hills. While your at it, why not take a selfie at *Gods Station'* too? Which is the local freight station by the train station. Hell is also a wonderful area for hiking and berry picking. Also explore Steinvikholm Castle, a historical site on a small island.

Røros

Røros is a historic mining town and part of UNESCO's World Heritage List. The old, wooden houses and the authentic atmosphere gives the place a special old charm. Try to visit during Rørosmartan (The Røros Market) or the Christmas Market in December. It takes approx 2,5-3 hour drive from Trondheim to Røros.

Oppdal

Oppdal is a mountain village just approx 2 hours drive from Trondheim, and is our version of swiss alps! Offering a breathtaking nature and a paradise for outdoor experiences. It is an excellent place for skiing, with first class alpine resorts and beautiful cross-country trails. During summer, it's perfect for hiking and climbing. You can also spot 'Moskus' around here. (Musk ox.)

Steinkjer

Two hours from Trondheim, Steinkjer is beautifully situated by the fjord and boasts many wonderful natural areas.

Known for its proximity to the prehistoric rock carvings at Bølareinen.

Gateway to the beautiful Skei area and Blåfjella-Skjækerfjella National Park.

Levanger

Famous for its charming town center and historical wooden architecture.

The town hosts an annual Midsummer Market with local crafts and food.

Nature and Scenic Areas

Innerdalen

Often called "Norway's most beautiful valley," it offers stunning hikes and pristine nature.

Dovrefjell-Sunndalsfjella National Park

Home to wild musk oxen (*moskus*), with excellent hiking trails and incredible mountain views.

Fosen Peninsula

Perfect for outdoor activities like hiking, cycling, and fishing.

Check out the beautiful beaches and coastal cliffs.

Selbu

Known for the Selbu mitten (Selbuvotter) and scenic lakes like Selbusjøen.

Snåsavatnet

One of Norway's largest lakes, great for fishing and kayaking.

Nearby Snåsa village is known for its Sami culture.

Islands and Coastal Areas

Hitra and Frøya (The famous salmon region)
Ideal for fishing and exploring the rugged coastline.

Tips: Try a seafood safari or visit the lighthouse at Sletringen, Frøya.

Vega Archipelago (just north of Trøndelag)
A UNESCO World Heritage Site known for its unique eiderdown harvesting culture. In a different region, but accessible from Trøndelag.

Stokkøya   Famous
for its beautiful sandy beach and Stokkøya Sjøsenter, offering food, design, and nature. (On photos, it can just as well seem like you might be in Southern Europe.)

Festningen

Local Traditions and Celebrations – Where the Past Meets the Present

Trondheim, as the historical heart of Norway, has a rich calendar of traditions, some of which are uniquely tied to its past. The city's history as a Viking hub and religious center still influences its festivals today, blending the old with the new.

Yes, Trøndere have a deep love for their traditions, and they take great pride in preserving and celebrating their cultural heritage. Whether it's local customs, historical events, or regional dialect, traditions in Trøndelag are a big part of daily life and community identity.

Here are a few examples of how much Trøndere value their traditions:

1. **Cultural Celebrations:**

17th May (Norwegian Constitution Day) is a huge event, and Trøndere go all out, donning their Trønderbunad, participating in parades, and celebrating with family and friends. On this day you are allowed, (or obliged?!) to eat as much ice cream and 'pølse' (sausage) as you possibly can. Then preferably go to the tivoli and take as many rides as you can, to vomit it all out again! (For obvious reasons!)

St. Olav Festival in Trondheim is one of the most important medieval festivals in Norway, celebrating the legacy of King Olav Haraldsson, the Viking king and saint. Trøndere embrace this mix of history and religion with open arms, attending concerts, historical reenactments, and medieval markets.

2. Connection to Nature:

Nature plays a huge role in Trønder traditions. Many Trøndere spend weekends in *hytta* (traditional cabins) to enjoy simple, rustic life, often skiing, hiking, or fishing. The outdoor life is sacred, especially in Trøndelag, where the region's natural beauty is an essential part of the local identity.

3. Bunad Tradition:

The Trønderbunad is a point of pride for both men and women in Trøndelag. Wearing the bunad on special occasions, such as 17th May and weddings, is a cherished tradition, and many families pass their bunads down through generations, making it a deeply personal symbol of heritage.

4. Traditional Food and Drinks:

Traditional foods like klippfisk (dried and salted cod), smalahove (sheep's head, though originally a culinary dish Western Norway, now also in Trøndelag), and local cheeses remain part of festive meals and gatherings, keeping culinary traditions alive. Let's not forget about 'sodd', as mentioned in the introduction, and 'fiskeboller i hvit saus' (fishballs blended in a white sauce).

Even karsk, the famous Trønder mix of coffee and moonshine, is part of their local tradition, especially in rural areas. Or instead of coffee, with tea (Te knert). While not as widely practiced today, it remains a quirky symbol of Trønder toughness and humor.

5. Strong Regional Identity:

Trønders are known for their strong connection to their regional identity, proudly speaking Trøndersk, celebrating local humor, and participating in regional events and festivals. Many Trønders enjoy embracing their roots and feel a deep connection to the history of their region, from its Viking past to its modern-day traditions.

6. Local Festivals and Traditions:

Beyond national celebrations, Trønders enjoy their own regional traditions, like Olsok (St. Olav's Day), which commemorates the death of King Olav and includes church services, concerts, and medieval-themed events.

Spelet på Stiklestad – is a famous historical play performed annually at Stiklestad, a village in Norway near the site of the Battle of Stiklestad, which occurred in 1030. The battle was pivotal in Norwegian history, marking the death of King Olaf II Haraldsson, later known as Saint Olaf, who played a key role in the Christianization of Norway. 30 km northeast of Trondheim. It is typically performed every summer, usually in late July, coinciding with the anniversary of the Battle of Stiklestad, which took place on July 29, 1030.

Elden på Røros – Elden in Røros refers to a unique, traditional fire festival celebrated in this UNESCO World Heritage town in central Norway. The event is typically held outside during summer, while celebrating local culture, traditions, and community spirit. Røros is about 2,5 hours drive from Trondheim.

Smaller community gatherings, such as local markeder (markets), cultural festivals, and rural traditions, are still held in high regard, bringing people together to celebrate their shared heritage.

Quirky, Local Traditions

The *utepils* is a sacred tradition, and commonly tied to the arrival of the sun after a long, dark winter. Once spring begins to peek through the clouds, and Trondheim's days start getting longer again, people gather for a celebratory drink (Trønder beer, *Dahls*) to mark both the end of the month's hard work and the return of the sun. It's a joyful moment when coworkers and friends meet at an outdoorsy pub, or outside in nature, not just to toast their paycheck but to embrace the brightness of the season, both literally and figuratively.

While this tradition is a fun way to mark the changing seasons, it also highlights the Trønder's knack for turning even the smallest occasion into a reason to socialize and enjoy life. The *utepils* is less about the pay and more about the mood: after months of winter darkness, a sunny payday beer is an excuse to embrace the lighter days ahead.

Skiing and Nature

Traveling in Trøndelag

Kaffe sup

Ut på tur – aldri sur

"Trønders are fiercely independent. They value their space and may not always express emotions in a way you're used to. This doesn't mean they don't care, it just means they show it differently."

— T

TRØNDERS' RELATIONSHIP WITH NATURE - IT'S PERSONAL

In Trondheim, nature isn't something you visit on weekends, it's a part of everyday life. Whether it's the fjords, the forests, or the rugged mountains, the outdoors beckons constantly. Trønders take immense pride in their surroundings, and the concept of "friluftsliv" (outdoor life) is central to their identity.

Friluftsliv – The Art of Doing Nothing Outdoors

For Trønders, the best way to appreciate nature is by simply being in it. You don't need to climb a mountain or run a marathon, just going for a walk in the woods, sitting by a lake, or enjoying a moment of silence in a cabin is considered a perfect way to unwind. This deep connection to the land runs through everything, from their conversations to their art, and of course, their mindset. That being said, Norwegians are in general very athletic and outdoorsy, in the sence that they do a lot without being competitive about it.

In Trondheim and the surrounding Trøndelag region, bærsanking (berry picking) and høst (harvest) are deeply rooted traditions tied to friluftsliv (outdoor life). These activities are part of the region's cultural identity, where locals spend time in nature, gather wild berries, and celebrate the seasonal changes.

Bærplukking (Berry Picking) in Trøndelag

Bærsanking is not just a practical activity but also an important social event. Throughout the summer and early autumn months, Trønders head into the forests and fields to collect wild berries such as blueberries, lingonberries, and cloudberries. This tradition reflects the Trønders' deep connection with nature and the joy of harvesting the fruits of the land. Many families will even turn their berry picking trips into an annual event, bringing children along to learn the skills and history of foraging.

Trøndelag's varied landscapes, ranging from forests to moors, offer an abundance of wild berries. Local guides and blogs often highlight the best spots for picking and offer tips on respecting nature while collecting. For example, it's important to ensure you leave enough berries behind for wildlife and to ensure that the picking is done sustainably.

Høstsanking (Harvesting) and Seasonal Gatherings

As autumn arrives, høstsanking kicks into full gear. This refers to the broader harvest season when locals gather fruits, vegetables, mushrooms, and herbs that have grown during the summer months. Trønders take pride in their seasonal harvests, which are often shared among families and communities. Autumn in Trondheim means not only berry-picking but also the harvest of wild mushrooms, root vegetables, and the preparation of local foods for winter storage.

The harvest is often accompanied by community gatherings, where food preservation traditions are passed down. Families might make jams, preserve vegetables, and create dishes like rakfisk (fermented fish) to ensure they have food through the long winter months.

Friluftsliv (Outdoor Life)

Both berry-picking and harvest activities are part of the broader *friluftsliv* tradition in Trøndelag. The Norwegian concept of friluftsliv, which loosely translates to "open-air living," involves spending time outdoors, regardless of the weather, to reconnect with nature and promote physical and mental well-being. For many Trønders, friluftsliv is not just a hobby; it's a way of life. Whether it's hiking, picking berries, or simply sitting by a fire in the forest, it's about embracing the natural world around you.

This connection to nature is strongly tied to Trøndelag's history and way of life. The region's rugged landscapes and vast forests have always been essential to survival, making activities like berry-picking and harvest not just recreational but also essential for life in the region.

Together, bærplukking, høstsanking, and friluftsliv form an important part of the Trøn-der lifestyle, encapsulating a sense of community, tradition, and respect for nature. Whether you're a local or a visitor, these activities offer a unique way to experience the beauty and bounty of the Trøndelag region.

Cabin Culture

Every Trønder dreams of having their own "hytte" (cabin). Located in remote areas or hidden in the mountains, cabins are places of solace and reflection. They're a retreat from modern life, with no distractions, just the sound of the wind and the crackle of a fireplace. Weekends at the cabin are a common escape, and for many, it's a family tradition passed down through generations. (Obviously, times are changing here too. Modern cabins are becoming a welcoming part to the new generation!)

For more insights into these traditions, I advice you to explore resources from local tourism sites or guides on Norwegian outdoor life like Visit Trondheim, Trondheim Turistforening and Friluftsliv Norge.

Fjellvetttreglene (The Mountain Safety Rules)

In Norway, not just Trøndelag, there is no specific law about the weather, but there are various laws and regulations concerning safety and responsibility when being outdoors, especially regarding weather conditions.

The Outdoor Life Act (Friluftsloven)

An important law in Norway for people who venture into nature is the Outdoor Life Act (Lov om friluftslivet). This law gives Norwegian citizens the right to access nature, and it emphasizes that people should take responsibility for their own safety, especially concerning weather and terrain conditions. The law does not impose specific requirements regarding weather but serves as a reminder that anyone venturing into nature should be knowledgeable about conditions and be prepared for changes in the weather.

Weather Conditions and Responsibility

Fjellvettreglene (the Mountain Safety Rules)

They are a set of guidelines developed by the Norwegian Trekking Association (Den Norske Turistforening, DNT) to ensure the safety of people venturing into the mountains. These rules are especially important in Norway, where the weather can change rapidly and the terrain can be challenging, even in summer months.

The Fjellvettreglene are designed to help hikers and outdoor enthusiasts make safe and responsible decisions in the mountains.

Here are the Fjellvettreglene (Mountain Safety Rules):

1. Plan your trip and let someone know where you're going.

2. Adapt the trip to your abilities and the conditions.

3 Pay attention to weather and avalanche warnings.

4.Be prepared for storms and cold, even on short trips.

5. Bring the necessary equipment to help yourself and others.

6.Choose safe routes. Recognize avalanche-prone terrain and unsafe ice.

7. Use a map and compass. Always know where you are.

8.Turn back in time; there is no shame in turning around.

9.Save your energy and seek shelter if necessary.

World Ski Championship 2025 – Trondheim's Time to Shine (Or Freeze)

Welcome to Trondheim 2025, where locals will soon get to watch athletes from around the globe experience the true meaning of "chilly reception." As Trondheim prepares to host the World Ski Championship, Trønders are buzzing with excitement... well, as much as Trønders can buzz, which means a few mild nods and perhaps a slightly more animated "ja ja." No, seriously—we're all beyond excited and ridiculously proud to show off Trøndelag during the World Championship! And I promise you, there'll be more than just polite nods. With alcohol flowing freely, expect the best conversations, the biggest smiles, and even the shyest souls to come out of their shells!

The 2025 FIS Nordic World Ski Championships (Ski VM) are set to take place at the Granåsen Ski Centre in Trondheim. (Though this book is likely published after the championships.) Granåsen, located just a few kilometers outside the city center, is Trondheim's main winter sports venue, well-equipped with ski jumps, cross-country trails, and facilities for hosting large-scale events.

The venue has hosted major events before, so Trondheim is preparing to warmly (or perhaps frostily) welcome international athletes and spectators to enjoy the excitement, and likely some gusty, snowy winds!

And let's not forget the ski mascot—Snedi! Yet another delightfully weird Trønder word that probably makes zero sense to outsiders but fills us with an unreasonable amount of pride.

The Preparation: Trondheim-Style

The lead-up to this event is something to behold. All across the city, Trønders have been preparing the only way they know how: by intensifying weather discussions. Talk of snowfall, wind patterns, and icy sidewalks has reached epic proportions. Meanwhile, shop windows feature mannequins dressed in the latest ski attire, all in black, of course, because heaven forbid anyone stands out in winter.

The Athletes' Guide to Surviving Trønder Conditions

For the athletes, Trondheim's unique conditions will present a test like no other. Not only must they navigate the terrain, but also the constant threat of getting caught in a "surkel" (snowy wind that seems to come from all directions). The trick is to angle your body at approximately 45 degrees, just to stay upright. If they survive this, they're considered honorary Trønders.

Local Cheers: The Trønder Way

Expecting Trønders to cheer and wave flags with abandon might be a tad optimistic. Trønders are more likely to be found standing stoically along the ski tracks, holding their coffee thermoses like battle swords. Cheering usually sounds like, "Ja, bra det, heia! followed by a sip of coffee and a conversation about how today's snow doesn't hold a candle to the blizzards of certain spesific years. Any athlete looking for loud cheers might just need to make peace with applause that's mostly done with gloved hands and a faint nod.

Post-Race Reflections and after-ski

After the races, the city will likely come together to celebrate the victories in true Trønder style: with a local stew (sodd or fish soup, preferably served lukewarm), a steady flow of *Karsk*—the classic Trønder drink made from coffee and moonshine—or *aquavit* for the more refined palate, all topped off with an abundance of beer. Because in Trondheim, no celebration is complete without it! Expect the streets to be alive with tales of snowy misadventures, as locals debate who managed to stay upright on the slopes and who had to make use of the snowbank. Athletes might leave Trondheim with a newfound love for coziness, wrapped in layers of wool, and a quiet promise to ski only in warmer, less snowy places from now on.

Ultimately, visitors to Trondheim during Ski VM can expect an unforgettable mix of outdoor excitement, cozy indoor traditions, and a hearty and proud welcome from Trønders that may be subtle but is warm at heart. And if they survive the ski events and the chill, they'll take home the true Viking bragging rights!

Granåsen SKI VM 2025

After-Ski (and What it Really is?)

The concept of after-ski (or après-ski in French, which means "after ski") is often associated with Scandinavian ski culture, and while it's not exclusively a Norwegian invention, Norway certainly played a significant role in popularizing the tradition.

Origins of Après-Ski
The idea of socializing after a day of skiing has roots in Alpine ski culture, particularly in France and Switzerland, where ski resorts were developed early in the 20th century. The French term après-ski became widely used to describe the social activities that take place after a day on the slopes, including eating, drinking, and dancing.

Norway's Contribution
Norway, however, has had a strong influence on the development of skiing as a sport, particularly in the early 20th century, when Norwegian skiers dominated international competitions and helped shape modern skiing techniques. Norway's ski culture is deep-rooted, and its ski resorts in Trønderland, they have embraced après-ski as part of the overall experience, combining it with Norwegian traditions of enjoying cozy gatherings in cabins, serving hearty food, and drinking gløgg (mulled wine) or beer or yes, stronger liquer is permitted too. Up in the slopes, people tend to gather in the ski resort cafeterias, drinking beer or even (*heimbrent*)*karsk*! – Before heading home to continue their after-ski soirée.

In Norway, après-ski tends to be more about warmth and comfort gathering in a cabin or lodge after skiing to enjoy some good food, drink, and lively conversation. While it may not have been coined in Norway, the country's ski culture certainly emphasizes the after-ski experience, especially in the colder months.

Modern Après-Ski

In contemporary ski resorts, both in Norway and abroad, après-ski has become a vibrant part of the ski culture, often with live music, dancing, and themed parties. Ski resorts in Norway have embraced this as a way to round off the skiing experience, combining Norwegian coziness with the fun and social aspects of après-ski.

So, while Norway may not have "invented" après-ski, it certainly contributed to its spread and development, especially with its strong connection to skiing culture and a love for socializing after a day on the slopes.

"It goes as it goes, and usually it goes just fine – at least if you have a coffee cup."
— T (Inspired by multiple Norwegians).

TRØNDELAG - WHERE EVERYONE IS LOW-KEY FAMOUS

The thing about Trønders is that they don't brag, ever. You could be having a casual conversation with someone in a Trondheim café, and only later find out they're a famous athlete, rock star, or world-class artist. It's not that Trønders don't know how to celebrate success, it's just that they'd rather get back to what really matters: sipping coffee, complaining about the weather, and planning their next trip to the cabin.

So the next time you find yourself in Trøndelag, don't be surprised if you run into a celebrity who doesn't act like one. In fact, you might not even realize you've met a famous Trønder until much later. But that's the beauty of Trønder culture: it's all about keeping things low-key, even when you're secretly a superstar.

FAMOUS TRØNDERS - PROOF THAT YOU CAN BE A SUPERSTAR EVEN IF YOU HATE SMALL TALK

While Trønders may seem like a humble bunch who prefer the quiet life, they've still managed to produce some serious stars. Whether it's music, politics, or football, Trøndelag's got its fair share of famous faces, though in true Trønder style, they probably won't brag about it. Here's just a small taste of a few.

Åge Aleksandersen – The Godfather of Trønderrock

If you want to understand the soul of Trøndelag, just listen to Åge Aleksandersen. This guy is basically the Bruce Springsteen of Trondheim. With hits like "Levva Livet" and "Lys og Varme," he's the soundtrack to every Trønder family gathering, wedding, or spontaneous road trip. His voice practically is the Trønder accent in musical form. You can't escape Åge in Trøndelag, nor would you want to, he's a legend. And even though his lyrics are about as subtle as a Viking raid, Trønders love him because he gets them: stoic, nostalgic, and just a little bit rock 'n' roll.

Odd Reitan – The King of Convenience (Stores)

Ever wondered why there are so many REMA 1000 stores in Norway? You can thank Odd

Reitan, a true Trønder who turned his love for low prices into a grocery empire. Odd is basically Norway's answer to Jeff Bezos, but with less drama and more budget-friendly bread rolls. His motto? "The simple is often the best," which could honestly be the unofficial slogan of Trønder culture. REMA 1000 is everywhere much like the unshakable optimism that tomorrow's weather might be better.

Roald Dahl – Yes, THAT Roald Dahl

Believe it or not, the beloved children's author Roald Dahl has roots in Trøndelag. While Dahl himself was born in Wales, his father hailed from Sarpsborg, and his mother was from Trondheim. So, yes, we can thank Trøndelag for giving us Charlie and the Chocolate Factory, Matilda, and The BFG. And you know what? If you've ever read Roald Dahl's dark, twisted humor, you might just see a bit of dry Trønder wit hiding between the lines. Coincidence? We think not.

Liv Ullman – Yes, THAT famous Hollywood Actress.

And also producer, director and writer, and what not!

Sure, she was Born in Japan, but her family moved back to Trondheim, where she grew up. Liv Ullmann is an internationally renowned actress and director, best known for her collaborations with Swedish filmmaker Ingmar Bergman. She's widely regarded as one of the greatest actresses in the world, with a career that spans over six decades, making her a true icon not just for Trondheim or Norway, but globally.

Marit Bjørgen – Ski Queen with Trønder Grit

Sure, the Oslo elite might get the spotlight, but don't sleep on Trøndelag's cross-country skiing stars. Marit Bjørgen, a skiing sensation who's won multiple World Championship medals, comes from this no-nonsense land of fjords and forests. Her tough-as-nails attitude on the track is pure Trønder spirit: no flashy celebrations, just quiet, unstoppable determination. She's the type who would win a gold medal and then go straight to the cabin to chop wood.

Erik Hoftun – The Silent Football Hero

Trondheim's Rosenborg football club is practically a religion here, and Erik Hoftun is its quiet god. As a legendary defender for both Rosenborg and the Norwegian national team, Hoftun wasn't flashy, he just got the job done, much like any good Trønder. While other football stars might go for dramatic post-game interviews, Hoftun would simply nod, shrug, and say something like "det gikk jo greit" (it went fine). Classic.

Astrid S – Pop Idol

Astrid S is famous for being a pop singer, songwriter, and musician with a distinct electro-pop style. She gained initial fame in 2013 as a contestant on the Norwegian version of Pop Idol, where she finished in the top five. Since then, she has achieved international recognition for her music, with hits such as "Hurts So Good," "Think Before I Talk," and "Emotion." Originally from rennebu, a small town close to Trondheim.

Carina Dahl – Performer and Media Personality

Carina is a Norwegian singer, songwriter, and television personality. She is primarily famous for her music career, with several pop and dance tracks that have gained popularity in Norway. Some of her notable songs include "I Don't Care," "Waste Your Time," and "Hold Me Close." In addition to her music, she has participated in the Norwegian edition of Melodi Grand Prix multiple times, which is the national selection for the Eurovision Song Contest. Carina is also known for her lively and outgoing personality, which has made her a well-known figure in Norwegian entertainment, both as a performer and as a media personality.

Johannes Høsflot Klæbo – is the most notable current ski star from Trondheim, recognized as one of Norway's top cross-country skiers. Known for his sprinting prowess and tactical finesse, Klæbo has won numerous World Championships and 11 Olympic medals since he emerged as a top competitor in 2017. With 6 of the medals from the Olympics in 2026! Growing up and training in Trondheim, he has a strong local fan base and has been a prominent figure in the 2025 World Ski Championships, which Trondheim hosted.

Marit Moum Aune – A renowned Norwegian Actress & Theater Director.

She is known for her work in both theater and film. She is particularly recognized for her performances in Norwegian theater productions. Aune has been involved in a range of artistic projects, including acting in plays and participating in television productions. She is associated with Norway's theater scene and is noted for her ability to take on a variety of roles, demonstrating her versatility as an actress. While she may not be a household name internationally, she is respected within Norwegian cultural and artistic circles.

Mona Grudt - The Trønder Who Won the World (Miss Universe 1990.)

The pride of Trøndelag is Mona Grudt. She did something unimaginable and won the title, Miss Universe in 1990. Which means that at one point in history, the most beautiful woman on earth was a Trønder. This confuses a lot of people. Because Trønders are not exactly known for standing on a stage and shouting:

"Look at me! I'm Miss Universe!" That would be far too much fuss. A Trønder who wins Miss Universe is much more likely to shrug modestly and say something like: "Jaja... it went quite well." And judging by her calm and down-to-earth nature, that is probably exactly how Mona Grudt handled it too.

Gustav Magnar Witzøe – The Salmon Billionaire from the Billionaire Island: Frøya

Then there is the billionaire heir to the salmon empire SalMar. He comes from Frøya, which is not exactly known as the fashion capital of the world. Frøya is known for three things: 1.Wind 2.Fish 3.More wind.

Yet somehow, this windswept island produced a billionaire model. Which means somewhere on Frøya there is a fisherman saying: "We raised him on fish and storms. How did he end up in Vogue?" And here's the Trøndersk part: even as a billionaire model, Gustav is still humble, down-to-earth, and kind. He doesn't parade around in suits or yachts. He'll politely smile, wave, maybe even help out on a boat if asked. Because no matter how much money or fame you have, on Frøya the first question is always:

"Yes, yes, but do you help out with the boats?"

More Trønder Celebrities – Because Trøndelag Is Basically Norway's Talent Factory

While the world might look to Oslo for its glitzy stars, Trøndelag quietly keeps churning out an impressive array of talent. From the arts to sports, and even politics, this region seems to have a special knack for producing big names though true to Trønder style, most of them would rather enjoy a quiet coffee at the cabin than bask in the limelight. Let's take a look at a few more famous faces who've made their mark.

Trine Skei Grande – The No-Nonsense Politician

Trine Skei Grande is a prominent political figure who led Norway's Liberal Party (Venstre) and served as Minister of Culture and Education. Her roots are firmly planted in Trøndelag's soil, and like any good Trønder, she mastered the art of cutting through the nonsense. Known for her straightforward and practical approach to politics, Trine isn't one for grandstanding, she's more likely to get things done while giving you a look that says, "Let's not make this more complicated than it needs to be."

Bjarne Brøndbo – The Frontman of D.D.E. (Norwegian Party Legends)

If Åge Aleksandersen is the godfather of Trønderrock, Bjarne Brøndbo and his band D.

D.E. are the wild cousins who bring the party. Hailing from Namsos, Bjarne is known for his high-energy performances and raspy voice that could probably wake up a hibernating bear. D.D.E.'s songs, like "Det går likar no" (It's Getting Better Now) are staples at every Norwegian party, and if you haven't sung along to one of their anthems while slightly tipsy at a summer festival, are you even Norwegian? Trønders may not love to show emotions, but when D.D.E. hits the stage, even the most stoic among them can't resist shouting the lyrics at the top of their lungs.

Ida Jenshus – The Country Music Star with Trønder Soul

Ida Jenshus is Norway's answer to a country music star, except instead of Nashville, she grew up in Steinkjer. She's won multiple Spellemannprisen awards (Norwegian Grammys), and her blend of Americana and folk-rock has won her a loyal following. With her soulful voice and introspective lyrics, Ida brings a touch of Americana to the fjords. But make no mistake—no matter how many country tunes she sings, she's still Trønder through and through, probably preferring a quiet hike in the woods to any flashy red-carpet events.

Petter Northug – The Controversial Cross-Country Skiing Legend

If cross-country skiing had a rock star, it would be Petter Northug. Born in Mosvik, Petter's not just a champion—he's the champion, with two Olympic gold medals and numerous World Championship titles. But his legacy isn't just about skiing; it's about his larger-than-life personality. Petter is known for his cocky attitude, epic finishes, and ability to stir up headlines. Whether he's dominating on the ski track or making controversial off-track statements, Northug has never been afraid of the spotlight. But, in true Trønder fashion, he probably still enjoys a low-key day at the cabin, despite his celebrity status.

Håkon Bleken – The Artistic Icon

Håkon Bleken, a celebrated painter from Trondheim, has been a key figure in Norwegian contemporary art for decades. His works, known for their striking use of color and emotion, often reflect the darker sides of society. While his paintings can be intense and thought-provoking, Bleken himself embodies the classic Trønder trait of understatement. He might be a world-renowned artist, but he still has that down-to-earth, unpretentious vibe that's as much a part of Trondheim as the Nidaros Cathedral.

TNT – The Internationally acclaimed hardrockband from Trønderland

TNT is one of the most internationally successful rock bands to come out of Trøndelag, and particularly Trondheim. Formed in the early 1980s, the band became known for its high-energy blend of melodic hard rock and glam metal and for the astonishing guitar skills of Ronni Le Tekrø. TNT was formed in 1982 by guitarist Ronni Le Tekrø together with vocalist Dag Ingebrigtsen, who was already well known in Trondheim's music scene. The band quickly became one of Norway's most exciting rock acts. Their debut album TNT made waves nationally, but it was their later albums that would launch them internationally.

Gøran Sørloth – The Football Star Who Quietly Dominated

Gøran Sørloth is a former Norwegian footballer who made a name for himself playing as a striker for Rosenborg and the national team. Born in Kristiansund but raised in Trondheim, Sørloth was part of the golden era of Rosenborg football in the 1990s. His son, Alexander Sørloth, has since followed in his footsteps, becoming a top footballer in Europe. Like his father, Alexander embodies the Trønder spirit, quietly hardworking, letting his performance on the field do the talking.

Tre Små Kinesere - The Sound of Everyday Trøndelag

If you want to talk about truly Trøndersk music, it's impossible not to mention Tre Små Kinesere — one of the most beloved bands ever to come out of Trondheim. The band was formed in 1988 by Øystein Hegge, Ulf Risnes, and Baard Slagsvold. What made them stand out immediately was something quite unusual at the time: they sang pop songs in the Trondheim dialect. In the late 1980s and early 1990s, this was almost revolutionary. Most Norwegian pop music was either in English or in standard Norwegian. Tre Små Kinesere instead leaned fully into the Trønder sound, relaxed, witty, and slightly mischievous.

Motorpsycho - The Cult Band That Became a Legend

If there is one band that represents the restless, experimental, slightly eccentric creative spirit of Trondheim, it might very well be Motorpsycho. Formed in 1989 in Trondheim, Motorpsycho began as a noisy alternative rock band but quickly evolved into something much harder to categorize. Over the decades they have blended psychedelic rock, progressive rock, jazz, indie rock, and even folk, creating a musical universe entirely their own.

The core of the band has long been Bent Sæther and Hans Magnus Ryan (often called *Snah*), who together built one of the most respected rock catalogs in Europe.

DumDum Boys - From Punk Beginnings to Norwegian Rock Royalty

No chapter about Trøndelag's musical exports would be complete without DumDum Boys — one of Norway's most iconic rock bands and a cornerstone of the Trondheim music scene. The band formed in Trondheim in the mid-1980s and quickly became one of the defining Norwegian rock bands of the late 80s and 90s. At the center of the band is the charismatic frontman Kjartan Kristiansen, whose voice and personality became synonymous with Norwegian rock. DumDum Boys actually grew out of a punk band called Wannskrækk, which had already built a strong underground following in Trondheim. When they reinvented themselves as DumDum Boys in 1985, their sound evolved into something more melodic but still energetic — a powerful blend of rock, catchy hooks, and sharp Norwegian lyrics. Their breakthrough came with the album Splitter Pine, which became a massive success in Norway.

Arve Tellefsen - From Trondheim to the World Stage

If Trøndelag has given the world rock bands, explorers, and ski champions, it has also given the world one of its most celebrated violinists: Arve Tellefsen. Born in Trondheim in 1936, Tellefsen became one of Norway's most internationally respected classical musicians. His career has taken him to the great concert halls of the world, where his violin playing is known for its warmth, lyricism, and unmistakable Nordic tone. Even with international fame, Arve Tellefsen has always carried a certain Trøndersk warmth and humility. His concerts often include Norwegian folk melodies alongside classical repertoire, reflecting a deep connection to Norwegian musical traditions.

Kjell Erik Killi Olsen – A Renowned Norwegian Visual Artist.

He is known for his distinctive and often surreal paintings and sculptures. Yes, he is originally from Trondheim, born in 1952. His work is characterized by vivid colors, fantastical figures, and dreamlike, sometimes grotesque, themes. He explores existential and psychological concepts through his art, creating images that can be unsettling yet captivating. Killi Olsen gained international recognition in the 1980s, and his works have been exhibited widely in galleries and museums across Europe and the Americas. One of his most famous pieces is Salamandernatten (The Salamander Night), a large-scale installation with 72 surreal, human-like sculptures, which has been exhibited in multiple locations. He is celebrated in Trondheim, and his connection to the city is evident through various exhibitions and contributions to its cultural life. Among them the exceptional art gallery: 'K.U.K'.

Erlend Loe – A Norwegian Author, Screenwriter, and Film Critic.

He was indeed born in Trondheim. He is best known for his quirky, humorous writing style, often blending satire, absurdity, and existential themes. One of his most famous novels is Naiv. Super (1996), a story about a young man experiencing an existential crisis and seeking meaning in life. Apart from novels, Erlend Loe has written children's books, screenplays, and worked on several film and television projects. He is considered one of Norway's most influential contemporary authors.

Anne B. Ragde is a well-known Norwegian Author.

She is particularly famous for her family saga Berlinerpoplene (The Berlin Poplars), which became a huge success both as a book and a TV series in Norway. The Berlinerpoplene series follows the Neshov family and explores themes of family dynamics, secrets, and rural life in Norway. The books have been praised for their rich storytelling and vivid portrayal of Norwegian rural culture. Anne B. Ragde was born in Odda, Hordaland, but she grew up in Trondheim. She has a strong connection to Trondheim, where she has lived much of her life. Ragde has written across various genres, including novels, children's books, and crime fiction, and she has received several literary awards for her work. Her success with Berlinerpoplene has made her one of Norway's most popular contemporary authors.

Terje Tysland – The Voice of Trøndelag and Legend.

He is actually from Namsos, a town in Trøndelag county, about 200 km north of Trondheim. He's a well-known figure in the Trøndersk rock scene and one of Norway's classic rock artists, often associated with Trondheim because it's the cultural heart of Trøndelag. Tysland's style blends rock with Trøndersk dialect, folk elements, and a bit of country flair, perfectly capturing that distinct Trønder vibe! Terje and Åge Aleksandersen formed the band Prudence, a key moment that is often credited as the birth of Trønder rock.

Hans Rotmo – A Well-Known Musician, Songwriter, and Actor

He is from Verdal in Trøndelag, Norway, which is just an hour drive from Trondheim. He became famous for his satirical songs and folk music, often focusing on themes related to Norwegian rural life and Trønder culture. His distinct dialect and humor, reflect his Trønder roots, and he's widely regarded as an important cultural figure in the region.

Anne Krigsvoll – An Actress Hailing from Hitra.

She has been active in theater and film. Anne Krigsvoll is best known for her work in the Norwegian entertainment industry, particularly her involvement with various theater productions.

Her career spans both stage and screen, and she has become a recognized name in Norwegian cultural circles, especially in connection with performances that often explore the dynamics of Norwegian society and its challenges.

Ingrid Bolsø Berdal – A Well Known Actress from Inderøy.

Ingrid holds a significant place in both the national and international acting scene. A well renowned character-based actress. You may have seen her in Hercules (2014) as one of the Amazon warriors, playing alongside 'The Rock'.

Mikkel Storleer Eriksen & Tor Erik Hermansen – Stargate Music Productions.

These two music producers are from Trondhiem, but live in LA. They gained international fame for their work with artists like Beyonce, Rihanna and Katy Perry. Shaping the sound of modern pop music. Their roots in Trøndelag have certainly contibuted to their unique style and success.

In the grand scheme of things, Trønders might not seek the limelight, but their contributions to Norwegian culture are undeniable. From Viking warriors to world-class musicians, these stoic Northerners have a habit of excelling while pretending they're just going with the flow. And even though they'll never admit it, Trønders are kind of a big deal.

Munkholmen

Old Nidaros: Norway's Not-So-Secret Pretender to the Throne

Once, long ago, Trondheim was the capital of Norway. Kings were crowned, Viking ships bobbed in the fjord, and everyone agreed this was the center of the universe. But times changed. Royalty packed up for Christiania, (Oslo) and Trondheim gracefully let it slide, probably muttering, "Fine, but you'll be back."

Fast forward a millennium, and guess what? Trondheim is looking suspiciously like it's ready for its comeback tour. This city has been quietly transforming into the northernmost cultural hub of Europe. It's got everything a capital needs, minus the traffic jams and existential dread of Oslo commuters.

For starters, the art scene here isn't just thriving; it's practically breakdancing. Galleries and museums keep multiplying, offering everything from ancient relics to modern masterpieces. There's even an outdoor graffiti tour, which lets you pretend you're an art connoisseur while strolling through Trondheim's coolest back alleys.

Then there's the food. Trondheim doesn't just feed you; it romances your taste buds. Forget lutefisk nightmares; this is a city of Michelin-starred restaurants, Nordic fusion dishes that look like edible art, and seafood that's so fresh it probably swam here faster than your boat. They don't just serve food, they serve experiences.

Oh, and don't get us started on the music scene. Whether you're into jazz, punk, or something so experimental it sounds like robots having an argument, Trondheim has a stage for it. Combine that with NTNU's science and tech wizardry, and you've got a city that can rock out and reinvent the wheel. Who else can claim that?

So here's the thing: Trondheim is becoming too good at being awesome. It's almost like the city is softly humming, "What if we just... took the throne back?" And honestly, why not? Oslo has had its turn. It's all bureaucrats and high-rise glass boxes down there. Trondheim, meanwhile, has heart, culture, and a no-nonsense attitude.

Trondheim is a hidden gem in the art world, and its growing popularity among art connoisseurs and artists can be credited to several unique factors:

1. A vibrant and accessible art scene
Trondheim offers a dynamic mix of traditional and contemporary art spaces.

2. Historical backdrop meets modern creativity
Trondheim has an undeniable charm with its historic architecture, like the iconic Nidaros Cathedral, blending with its modern urban vibes. This juxtaposition inspires artists and provides a visually stunning setting for exhibitions, installations, and performances.

3. Graffiti and street art revolution
The city embraces street art like a true rebel. The Trondheim Graffiti Art Walk has become a must-see for art lovers, showcasing bold, colorful, and thought-provoking murals that adorn the city's walls.

4. Strong educational and cultural foundations
Trondheim is home to NTNU and other institutions that foster creativity and innovation. Programs in fine art, design, and architecture contribute to the city's steady stream of emerging talent. Add to this the many cultural events and workshops hosted throughout the year, and it's no wonder artists flock here.

5. A thriving gallery and museum scene
In addition to big-name institutions, smaller independent galleries and artist-run spaces thrive here, providing platforms for both established and up-and-coming artists. Events

like Trondheim Open invite the public into artist studios, breaking down the barriers between creators and admirers.

6. Festivals and international appeal

Events like the Kosmorama Film Festival, Trondheim Jazz Festival, and various contemporary art exhibitions attract international visitors. These festivals bring an infusion of global ideas while spotlighting Trondheim's local talent.

7. Art meets technology

Trondheim's reputation as a hub of innovation, courtesy of its tech-savvy population, has led to intriguing collaborations between art and technology. From digital installations to interactive media, artists in Trondheim are pushing boundaries and redefining what art can be.

8. A nurturing environment for artists

Unlike larger, more competitive cities, Trondheim provides a supportive environment for artists. Affordable studio spaces, grants, and an engaged audience make it an appealing base for creators looking to focus on their craft.

9. Authenticity and Quirkiness

Perhaps what makes Trondheim truly special is its blend of authenticity and playfulness. The city doesn't try to imitate larger art hubs, it embraces its unique character, fostering a creative environment that values originality over pretension.

For artists and art lovers alike, Trondheim is a city that feels both accessible and inspiring, offering a mix of tradition, innovation, and a good dose of Nordic charm.

The Trønders aren't saying they're coming for the crown (yet). But if you squint, you can almost see the ghosts of Viking kings smiling from the Nidaros Cathedral, like, "Yeah, it's about time." Let's not call it a coup. Let's call it... destiny.

So, with all this buzzing art, food, music, and brainpower, maybe it's time to ask: should Trondheim reclaim its rightful throne as Norway's capital? Oslo's had a good run, but let's face it, when was the last time anyone felt genuinely excited about yet another glassy fjord-front building or overpriced coffee?

Trondheim, on the other hand, has soul. It's got history, quirkiness, and a stubborn determination to prove that the middle of Norway is really where the magic happens. So, maybe it's time for the Trønders to dust off their crowns and stage a (peaceful) coup. The northernmost cultural hub in Europe deserves nothing less.

Trøndere vs. the Rest of Norway: A Playful Comparison

When it comes to Norwegians, there's no denying that each region has its unique personality, quirks, and stereotypes. Trøndere, of course, hail from the heart of Norway. From their distinct dialect to their pragmatic yet warm-hearted nature, to their laid-back funny humor. Let's have a look into the playful comparison of Trøndere versus the rest of Norway.

1. The Dialect and Humor

Trøndere are famous for their distinct accent and unique expressions. While the rest of Norway might struggle to understand a full conversation with a Trønder, locals enjoy playing with their rich vocabulary, which includes words like "fæst" (party) and "sørringa" (southerners). In contrast, other regions, like Oslo or Bergen, might sound a little more polished or lyrical, but Trøndere take pride in being direct and sometimes, let's admit it, quite blunt. Humor is a big part of Trøndelag culture, with quick-witted jokes and playful banter filling family gatherings and social events.

Rest of Norway: Polished politeness with a sprinkle of sarcasm.
Trøndere: Blunt, honest, and a touch of mischievous humor.

2. Work Ethic and Practicality

Trøndere are known for their solid work ethic, though they do it with a grin and a bit of humor. Whether it's working the land, hauling in the catch, or running a business, they get the job done, and they don't mind rolling up their sleeves to do it. But here's the secret: they make it look effortless. They know how to work hard, but they also know how to kick back and enjoy life. When the work's done, it's time for a good coffee and a laugh, and maybe a nap (don't tell anyone).

Meanwhile, the rest of Norway, whether from the bustling coast of Bergen or the fjord-filled villages of the West, might be more into taking things slow, savoring life at a relaxed pace. But no worries, The Trønders balance it out, work hard, but always with a sense of ease. Efficient? Sure. But they still know how to enjoy the ride.

3. Regional Pride vs. National Integration

Trøndere take great pride in their region, from their rich history to their place as a hub for innovation and creativity. They often joke that Trøndelag is the "centre of Norway," and, to be fair, they're not entirely wrong given Trondheim's historic significance as the old capital and seat of kings. Other regions, such as Oslo and Bergen, have a more centralized, national focus, but Trøndere delight in embracing their local identity.

Rest of Norway: Focused on national culture.
Trøndere: Embrace regional roots, history, and local traditions fiercely.

4. Cuisine and Traditions

Food-wise, Trøndere have a reputation for being adventurous yet traditional. You'll find specialties like rakfisk (fermented fish) and klubb (a hearty potato dumpling dish), which might not appeal to everyone but are celebrated in local culture.

Rest of Norway: More diverse, from refined dining to simple comfort food.
Trøndere: Hearty, traditional, and a touch more rustic.

5. Festivals and Social Gatherings

In Trøndelag, social gatherings are a mix of tradition and good times. They may involve a bit more structured participation, whether it's dancing around a fire or singing folk songs, but Trøndere ensure there's plenty of laughter and food to go around. Other regions, like Northern Norway or Southern coastal areas, might lean more toward modern festivities or outdoor activities.

Rest of Norway: Modern festivals with variety.
Trøndere: Traditional yet fun-filled with a touch of nostalgia.

6. Innovation vs. Tradition

While Trøndere deeply value their traditions, they are also known for being forward-thinking. From tech startups to environmental projects, they embrace innovation and change, while still maintaining respect for their roots. Conversely, regions like Østlandet may prioritize larger metropolitan trends and more global outlooks.

Rest of Norway: Focus on larger metropolitan or global innovations.
Trøndere: A perfect balance of tradition and modernity.

7. Stereotypes and Identity

Trøndere have a reputation for being independent and loyal to their land. Whether battling trolls in the forests or navigating the practicalities of a rugged coastline, their strength comes from the land they've cultivated for generations. Other regions might place more emphasis on social networks or cultural festivals, but Trøndere tend to be a bit more self-reliant.

Rest of Norway: Strong community focus and social gatherings.
Trøndere: Independent, resilient, and rooted in their local identity.

INTERNATIONAL
TRONDHEIM
INTERNATIONAL NEWS

TRONDHEIM
INTERNATIONAL NEWS
RISING
TO FAME

TRONDHEIM
INTERNATIONAL

T.Winther

TRONDHEIM RISING TO INTERNATIONAL FAME

Trondheim: From hidden gem to international darling

Once upon a time, Trondheim was just another sleepy Norwegian town with cobblestone streets, a towering cathedral, and more weather than it knew what to do with. Fast forward to today, and the city is basking in a moment of glory, rising from under the radar to claim its rightful spot on the global map, and not just for its wintery allure. Trondheim is now strutting its stuff on the world stage for its music, food, and science. Who would've thought?

The Music Scene: From black metal to breathtaking harmonies to international rock stars.

Trondheim has always had a musical soul, but lately, it's been tuning up for international stardom. Whether it's the haunting riffs of black metal that echo through its fjords or the dreamy indie sounds coming from student dorms, the city has become a melting pot of musical talent.

One key player in this crescendo is NTNU's Jazzlinja, the prestigious jazz conservatory. For decades, it's been churning out musicians so talented they make the northern lights look like a dull bulb.

And don't even get us started on the festival scene. Trondheim Calling, the city's answer to SXSW, is where emerging artists come to strut their stuff, and music fans flock like seagulls to a dropped waffle. It's loud, it's vibrant, and it's distinctly Trønder.

Foodie Heaven: Where farm meets fjord

Trondheim's culinary scene has undergone a transformation that can only be described as delicious. Long gone are the days when lutefisk was the only exotic offering. Now, Trondheim is a certified foodie paradise, with Michelin-starred restaurants and chefs who treat local ingredients with the reverence of Viking relics.

Take *Credo,* for example, where the chef might serve you a carrot so exquisitely prepared it brings tears to your eyes. *Fagn, To Rom & Kjøkken* or *Troll*, where traditional Nordic flavors are given a cheeky modern twist. Trondheim's farmers and fishers have also joined the movement, delivering produce fresher than the mountain air.

And let's not forget the beer! Trondheim's craft breweries are brewing up a storm, giving hipsters everywhere something new to Instagram. Local favorites like E.C. Dahls and Austmann Brewery are putting Trondheim on the map, one frothy pint at a time.

Science: Nerds rule here

If music and food weren't enough, Trondheim is also flexing its brainpower. NTNU (Norwegian University of Science and Technology) is the city's crown jewel, where brilliant minds come together to invent the future. Trondheim's scientists are making breakthroughs in renewable energy, AI, and medicine, making the rest of us feel quite inferior as we try to assemble IKEA furniture. "And yes! We have Nobel Prize winners here too, and we're damn proud of it!"

The city's tech scene is buzzing too. Trondheim is home to SINTEF, one of Europe's largest independent research organizations, and a growing number of startups. Whether it's self-driving boats or carbon-capture technology, Trondheim's innovators are working hard to save the planet while we're busy scrolling TikTok.

A city on the rise

So, there you have it. Trondheim has evolved from a quaint Scandinavian stopover to a bona fide cultural and scientific hub. With its symphony of music, culinary delights, and groundbreaking innovations, it's safe to say Trondheim is no longer content to be Norway's best-kept secret. Instead, it's shining, or maybe lightly drizzling on the world stage.

And let's be honest: isn't it a bit satisfying to watch the world finally catch on to what the Trønders have known all along? This little corner of Norway is pretty darn amazing.

Afterword

A Fond Farewell to Trønderland

As we wrap up this whimsical journey through Trønderland, I hope you've not only gained insight into the rich culture of Trondheim, a bit of Trøndelag and its people, but also found a few chuckles along the way. The Trøndere are a unique blend of humor, history, and heartfelt connection to their land. A combination that is as warming as a cup of freshly brewed coffee on a brisk winter morning.

We've wandered through the charming streets of Bakklandet, marveled at the magnificent Nidaros Cathedral, and embraced the quirky nuances of the local dialect. We've encountered legends of the past and present, and celebrated the everyday joys of Trønder life, where a simple greeting can be both a warm welcome and a cryptic puzzle, and where the weather remains a timeless topic of conversation.

As with any journey, it's not just about the destinations but the stories we gather along the way. Whether you're a native Norwegian or a curious visitor, I hope this book has sparked your curiosity to dig a little deeper into the vibrant culture of Trøndelag. Embrace the humor found in dry wit and deadpan expressions, and don't shy away from the warmth and genuine hospitality of the people.

So, the next time you find yourself in the capital of Trøndelag or Trønderland in general, take a moment to soak it all in: the sound of laughter mingling with the aroma of coffee, freshly made waffles, the stories told over shared meals, and the calmness of nature in this beautiful region. Immerse yourself in the local traditions, celebrate the peculiarities, and above all, join in the conversations, be it about the weather, local legends, or the latest happenings in the community.

Things I'll Never Quite Get Used To (Even though I'm basically a trønder now)

Despite being practically a Trønder at this point, there are a few customs here that still leave me scratching my head.

1.The Mysterious Case of the Reclaimed Wine

I've mentioned this before, but it still baffles me. If someone brings me (the host) a bottle of wine to a dinner party I am hosting, you have to understand that, by the time the night wraps up, the same person who brought it is gathering it up, half-drunk, and bringing it back home, like it's a forgotten child. It's like some sort of party ritual I'll never understand. (It may be fair to say, this does not happen as frequently anymore, and not all Trønders follow this code!) That being said, I must add that, Trønders are warm-hearted, generous people, not at all stingy. They are true givers.

2.Vær-Så-Gods (nøding)That Never Ends

Trønders are endlessly polite with their vær så god (you're welcome) but the paradox lies in thank you routines. (I was raised to always be polite and say thanks you and, sorry. Than just does not come at you in the same manner here in Trønderland!) I can't count the number of times I've sat at the table, stuffed, while everyone insists I take more food. "Just one more little taste!" Sure, if by little they mean a mountain of fårikål. Trønders won't stop until you're practically rolling home. In Trøndersk this is called nøding.

3.The Dugnad Dilemma

Ah, the infamous dugnad. The unspoken rule where suddenly the entire neighborhood comes together to clean up, paint, or fix something, with the same cheerful commitment of a military operation. I get it, community spirit and all, but every time I think I've escaped, there's another dugnad popping up like clockwork. And once you're in, you're in for life.

4. Trønder Logic: Making Friends and Losing Them with the Seasons

One of the things I still can't wrap my head around is this: you might meet and have a lovely chat with someone at a dugnad, but come the next day, it's like they've forgotten all about you! They look down, avoid eye contact, and act like you're strangers. Then, as soon as summer rolls in, it's all hugs and 'Hey, bestie!' again! It's like there's an unwritten rule about seasonal friendships that I'm clearly not in on!

5.This Weather Talk Obsession

I know Norwegians love talking about the weather, but here in Trondheim, it's like the national pastime. No matter where you are or who you're with, there's always time to talk about rain. Or wind. Or snow. Or all three, in the same hour. I've had whole conversations that never leave the subject of today's weather forecast, and then they tell me about tomorrow's too.

It's almost like a badge of honor when you can blend into these oddities and act like it's totally normal. But I have to admit, some of these traditions still leave me feeling like the eternal outsider. Maybe that's the secret of becoming a true Trønder, grinning and going along with it, even if you're still shaking your head inside.

After all my efforts to raise my kids with an international flair, they still came into this world in Trønderland, and there's no denying it, they're true Trøndere at heart! I guess I can't escape the fact that the love for coffee and the weather talk runs in their veins. And let's face it: I have become a fully bred Trønder myself! I've embraced the quirks, the traditions, and yes, even the weather gossip. I may have tried to sprinkle in a bit of worldly sophistication, but deep down, I'm just as ready to chat about the rain and sip on a strong cup of coffee as any born-and-bred local! It's time for the world to learn som *Trøndersk* sophistication now!

Trøndelag is the very best part of Norway, and I hope you will find it to be the best part too.

Thank you for tagging along on this wild and wonderful ride through Trondheim with me. May your future travels be filled with laughter, camaraderie, and plenty of good coffee. Until we meet again, keep your heart open, your umbrella handy, and your spirit ready for the unexpected. Skål to the Trønder way of life!

Tania x

Bonus: Essential Trønder Experiences

Bonus

Try a karsk: A potent blend of coffee and moonshine that's a Trønder classic. Be warned, it's strong enough to put hair on your chest.

Eat a Trondheim fish cake: These are a local delicacy and perfect for a quick snack. You'll find them in any grocery store in Trøndelag.

Economise: Be like a Trønder and make a packed lunch. *Matpakke,* with homemade bread, spread and coffee on a thermos.

THE AUTHOR

Tania Winther is a lifelong traveler, nomad, artist, and designer, with deep roots in Trøndelag. As a longtime observer of the Trønder way of life, Tania hopes this book will not only entertain but also shed light on the lesser-known quirks of the Trønders. Tania has spent years immersed in the region's distinct culture, exploring its art, history, and funny, heartwarming traditions. With a love for storytelling, she is trying to bring a unique perspective to the world of Trondheim and the Trønders, blending creativity with local knowledge. A true aficionado of the region's humor, warmth, and breathtaking landscapes, Tania has traveled extensively, and lived many places, but it's Trondheim that she now calls home.

Dig Deeper: Books & Resources

Trønderen – unik, sær og lækker – (The Trønder - Unique, odd and appealing) by Bjarne Håkon Hanssen og Marvin Wiseth.

Hel ved by Lars Mytting – Although it is about woodcutting, it captures the deep connection Norwegians have to nature and tradition.

Trøndere – nye folkelivsskildringer by Peter Egge.

Terje Bratberg has written several books on Trøndelag and Norwegian culture, with a particular focus on this region's history. "Terje Bratberg's books are important contributions to the understanding of Trøndelag and its role in Norwegian history and culture."

Books on identity and belonging (relevant to your themes):

Third Culture Kids: Growing Up Among Worlds by David C. Pollock og Ruth E. Van Reken – "Explores identity in globally mobile cultures."

Stranger in the Village by James Baldwin – "A powerful essay about being an outsider, which may resonate with some of your themes."

Home: A Short History of an Idea by Witold Rybczynski "A reflection on what 'home' means across cultures."

Norwegian Literature & Storytelling:

Olav Audunssøn i Hestviken by Sigrid Undset –"A medieval tale closely tied to Norway's past."

Kimen by Tarjei Vesaas – "A disquieting Norwegian novel that explores community and isolation."

Books on Janteloven & Scandinavian Social Norms:
A Fugitive Crosses His Tracks by Aksel Sandemose.
The Almost Nearly Perfect People by Michael Booth.
Lagom: The Swedish Art of Balanced Living by Linnea Dunne.
Scandinavians: In Search of the Soul of the North by Robert Ferguson.
Adrian Posepilt by Kristian Kristiansen (Set in 18th-century Trondheim, this novel follows the life of an orphaned boy as he navigates the challenges of the time, offering a vivid portrayal of historical Trøndelag.)
Language and Dialect:
Trøndersk språkhistorie: (Trøndersk Language History)
"Language Conditions in a Region," edited by Arnold Dalen, Jan Ragnar Hagland, and Stian Hårstad (This work examines the linguistic history of the Trøndersk dialect, with a focus on its development and regional variations.)
Snedig å koinn trøndersk by Tor Erik Jenstad "Clever to Know Trøndersk": (A semi-satirical guide that humorously explores the nuances of the Trøndersk dialect, giving the reader both entertainment and insight into local speech patterns.)
Historical and Cultural Studies:
The Heart of Norway: A History of the Central Provinces by Frank Noel Stagg.
Trøndelagens antropologi by Halfdan Bryn.
Travel and Exploration:
Travel Guide to Trondheim, Norway: Unforgettable Memories Await by Daniel K. Grinder.
A Frog in the Fjord: One Year in Norway by Lorelou Desjardins.
The Xenophobe's Guide to the Norwegians by Dan Elloway.
The Norway Way & Brown Cheese, Yes Please by Jenny K. Blake.
The Almost Nearly Perfect People: Behind the Myth of the Scandinavian Utopia by Michael Booth.
Neither Here nor There: Travels in Europe by american author: Bill Bryson.
The Social Guidebook to Norway by Julien S. Bourrelle.

Websites:

https://www.visitnorway.no/

https://visittrondheim.no/

https://trondelag.com/

https://norskfriluftsliv.no/

https://www.dnt.no/tt

THE UNOFFICIAL LAW OF TRØNDERISM

Unofficial. Unconstitutional. Unapologetically Trøndersk.
IN THE HIGH COUNCIL OF TRØNDERRIKET
Case No. Æ-12345-BRØL

COMPLAINT FOR RECOGNITION, RESPECT, AND LEGALIZATION OF TRØNDERSK HUMOR
(And Certain Rights to Say "Æ E KLAR" and mean absolutely nothing by It).
§ ARTICLE I – INTRODUCTION OF FACTS
§ 1.1 Trønders are known to mumble, grumble, and occasionally smile.
§ 1.2 The sacred response to any question, regardless of content or urgency, is *"Jaja"*.
§ ARTICLE II – CULTURAL PRESERVATION
§ 2.1 It is hereby declared illegal to make fun of the "trønderbart" unless you are in possession of one yourself.
§ 2.2 Use of Bokmål in serious discussion may result in a temporary ban from the Rema 1000 parking lot.
§ ARTICLE III – THE LANGUAGE CLAUSE
§ 3.1 "Æ" is a vowel.
§ 3.2 Trønderism is hereby declared a sacred, vowel-based language, primarily communicated through sounds, tone, and strategic silence.

§ 3.3 Full conversations may legally begin, end, and be sustained solely with: *"æh"*, *"mmm"*, *"jaja"*, *"uff da"*, and interpretive eyebrow movement.

§ **ARTICLE IV – CONSEQUENCES OF VIOLATION**

§ 4.1 Any Østlending who attempts to mimic the dialect shall be subject to 40 hours of mandatory sentence: *watching Rosenborg highlights with commentary by someone's uncle from Melhus.*

§ 4.2 Violation of the sacred art of *saying little but meaning a lot* may result in enforced exile to Oslo.

DECLARATION

WHEREFORE, Plaintiff requests this Honourable Court of Public Trønder Opinion to uphold the rights, rituals, and righteous sarcasm of all Trøndere, and to immediately implement *The Law of Trønderism* across all participating kommuner (and optional fjords).

DATED this 25th day of January, anno 2024

Respectfully submitted,

Tania Winther,

Unofficial Spokesperson for Trøndelands *Secret Humor Law*

Certified in Awkward Silence Management, Vowel-Based Dialogue, and Advanced Mmmm-Hmm Communication.

www.ingramcontent.com/pod-product-compliance
Lightning Source LLC
Chambersburg PA
CBHW060140150626
46550CB00015B/2201